COOLFARMING

Coolfarming

Turn Your Great Idea Into the Next Big Thing

PETER GLOOR

AMACOM AMERICAN MANAGEMENT ASSOCIATION
New York · Atlanta · Brussels · Chicago · Mexico City · San Francisco
Shanghai · Tokyo · Toronto · Washington, D. C.

Bulk discounts available. For details visit:
www.amacombooks.org/go/specialsales
Or contact special sales:
Phone: 800-250-5308
Email: specialsls@amanet.org
View all the AMACOM titles at: www.amacombooks.org

This publication is designed to provide accurate and authoritative information in regard to the subject matter covered. It is sold with the understanding that the publisher is not engaged in rendering legal, accounting, or other professional service. If legal advice or other expert assistance is required, the services of a competent professional person should be sought.

Library of Congress Cataloging-in-Publication Data

Gloor, Peter A. (Peter Andreas), 1961–
Coolfarming : turn your great idea into the next big thing / Peter Gloor.
   p. cm.
Includes bibliographical references and index.
ISBN-13: 978-0-8144-1386-9
ISBN-10: 0-8144-1386-2
1. Creative ability in business. 2. Technological innovations—Management. 3. New products—Management. I. Title.
HD53.G548 2010
658.5'75—dc22

                                                          2010005515

About AMA
American Management Association (www.amanet.org) is a world leader in talent development, advancing the skills of individuals to drive business success. Our mission is to support the goals of individuals and organizations through a complete range of products and services, including classroom and virtual seminars, webcasts, webinars, podcasts, conferences, corporate and government solutions, business books and research. AMA's approach to improving performance combines experiential learning—learning through doing—with opportunities for ongoing professional growth at every step of one's career journey.

Printing number
10 9 8 7 6 5 4 3 2 1

CONTENTS

ACKNOWLEDGMENTS

This book could never have been written without the help of a large and dedicated group of collaborative innovators. Tom Malone, Tom Allen, and Rob Laubacher have been mainstays of support at MIT for the last six years. More recently, Sandy Pentland, Daniel Olguin Olguin, and Ben Waber from the MIT Media Lab have provided invaluable support helping to make best use of their social badges. Hans Brechbuhl and M. Eric Johnson provided initial support for the project at the Dartmouth Tuck Center for Digital Strategies. Robin Athey, Thomas Schmalberger, and Adriaan Jooste were early role models of creators at Deloitte Consulting. Yan Zhao, Song Ye, Marius Cramer, and Scott Dynes were crucial in the development of earlier versions of Condor; Renaud Richardet, Hauke Führes, Jonas Krauss, Stefan Nann, and Marc Egger are doing a stellar job converting Condor into a real software product. Special thanks go to Jonas Krauss and Stefan Nann for independently developing new versions of the Web trend prediction system for stocks and movies, and to Stefan Nann, Jonas Krauss, Hauke Führes, and Kai Fischbach for being great COIN members of our software startup, galaxyadvisors.

Ken Riopelle, Francesca Grippa, Min-Hyung Kang, Marco DeMaggio, and Julia Gluesing are great contributors to our virtual COIN on COINs. Detlef Schoder, Kai Fischbach, Johannes Putzke, Daniel Oster, and Eric Esser from the University of Cologne make my stays there a real pleasure, providing great food for thought and the body. Casper Lassenius, Maria Paasivaara, Tuomas Niinimäki, and Shosta Sulonen are offering a similarly stimulating environment at the SoberIT group at Helsinki University of Technology (now part of Aalto University). Yared Kidane helped develop early insights on creative collaboration patterns. Superconnectors Pascal Marmier and Christoph Von Arb from Swissnex, the Swiss Scientific Consulate in Boston supply a great incubator for my COIN ideas. Scott Cooper was an inspiring sparring partner for developing early coolfarming ideas when we wrote the predecessor book, Coolhunting, together. I also would like to thank Stefan Nann, Kai Fischbach, Jonas Krauss, and Detlef Schoder for critical feedback and excellent suggestions on earlier versions of the manuscript. Thank you all, for over and over again providing the shoulders of giants to step onto to take my ideas to the next step! Without your assistance and creative help, this book would never have been possible.

COOLFARMING

1

How Do You Turn a Cool Idea into a Trend?

As special as Steve is, I think of Apple as a great jazz orchestra. Steve did a superb job of recruiting a broad and deep talent base. When a group gets to be that size, the conductor's job is pretty nominal—mainly attracting new talent and helping maintain the tempo, adding bits of energy here and there.[1]

　　—Michael Hawley, professional pianist/computer scientist/former Apple employee

WHY IS IT that Apple products are cool? Why is Steve Jobs cool? What if you could become cool, too? And what if you could make your own ideas cool? What if you could even turn them into the next big thing?

The good news is, there are indeed steps you can take to be cool, and to convert your ideas into a cool trend. This book addresses the basic questions of what the magic of cool is. It shows you how to "coolfarm" your ideas, how to make trends cool, and how to become cool yourself. *Coolfarming* tells how to convert creative dreams into cool products by enlisting the help of dedicated and passionate collaborators. *Coolfarming* is about how to get the "next big idea" off the ground.

So what is it that makes things cool? Cool things have four properties:

1. Cool things need to be *fresh and new*. We don't want yesterday's stale old ideas, but radically new and better ones. Apple is cool, Microsoft is not. Why? Apple has a unique knack for repeatedly coming up with beautiful new product concepts and designs that usher in new markets, first in computers with the Macintosh, then in digital music players with the iPod, and then in mobile phones with the iPhone. Microsoft has grown bigger in size and may be more profitable with its copycat strategy, but nobody has ever accused it of being cool—that's reserved for creators of radically new things. Microsoft's technology does the job, but it's clunky, arcane, and clogged with features that nobody wants. Apple, on the other hand, has consistently defined new markets with superbly designed, innovative products.

2. Cool things make us *part of a community*. They help us be with people like us. As psychologists and sociologists have found out, if given the chance, we want to be with as many people "like us" as possible—the more the merrier. Why did two million people trek to Washington's National Mall for the inauguration of President Barack Obama? Why did they stand in line for eight hours to personally attend Obama's swearing in and not just watch it on TV? Simple answer: It was the chance to be part of something cool and new, to witness change, jointly, with two million other like-minded souls. Even something as simple as owning the latest iPhone or BlackBerry makes the owner part of a community, a sister and brotherhood, with the token of entry being the coolest of handsets.

3. Cool things are *fun.* Just owning an iPhone is fun, if only because it is so well designed and looks so cool. Making calls and surfing the Web on an iPhone is fun; playing music on an iPod is fun. Going to a musical on Broadway is fun and relaxing. Drinking coffee in Starbucks is fun, too, not the least because every Starbucks customer is in good company with other people who are also enjoying a good cup of coffee in a relaxing atmosphere. It's not for nothing that Starbucks carefully selects and trains its baristas to provide a superior customer experience.

4. Finally, cool things give *meaning to our life.* Cool things make people feel good and happier. Owning a cool thing can become a goal all by itself, whether it is the new iPhone, the designer bag from Adidas, or the car we always wanted. Of course, owning a cool thing could also mean joining an activist group to fight global warming. For many people the thing that gives meaning to their lives is making the world a better place—the ultimate in cool.

Cool trends can only be created through the creativity of swarms. My previous two books, *Swarm Creativity* (Oxford University Press, 2006) and *Coolhunting* (AMACOM, 2007), introduced the idea of Collaborative Innovation Networks (COINs) and explained how to coolhunt. Coolhunting is the art and skill of chasing down cool trends by spotting the trendsetters collaborating in COINs. This book makes the bold leap to "coolfarming," explaining the steps that anybody can take to make cool trends happen. Obviously COINs cannot be mandated into action, and inventions cannot, by sheer force of will, be turned into new trends. Nevertheless, there are steps that the creator of a new idea or the enthusiastic very early adopter of a concept can take to increase the odds of turning the cool new thing into, indeed, a new trend.

The Four Steps of Coolfarming

This swarm-based innovation process happens in four steps:

STEP 1 The creator comes up with the cool idea.

STEP 2 The creator recruits additional members to form a Collaborative Innovation Network (COIN).

STEP 3 The COIN grows into a Collaborative Learning Network (CLN) by adding friends and family.

STEP 4 Outsiders join, forming a Collaborative Interest Network (CIN).

These four steps establish the most efficient engine of innovation, creating the innovations that continuously change our lives. This book is written for creators and COIN members. If you are looking for practical hands-on advice on how to carry your cool ideas over the tipping point, converting them into real trends, this book is for you.

CREATORS

In 1857, Eduard-Leon Scott de Martinville invented and patented the phonautograph in France. The phonautograph was an ingenious device to record the human voice using a system to encode black and white dots on a sheet of paper. Chances are you never have heard of de Martinville or his device. Right after he filed his patent, he was forgotten. The fame—and the riches—went to somebody else. Most likely you learned at school that Thomas Alva Edison, roughly thirty years later, invented the phonograph to record and play back music and sound. The question is, Why did Edison succeed when de Martinville failed? The answer: Edison was a coolfarmer and creator, de Martinville was not.

De Martinville had really clever ideas, but he was not able to get them across. His environment, his "swarm," his peer group in mid-nineteenth-century Paris refused to accept and embrace his innovation. Contrast this to Edison, who has an unbeatable track record as one of the most prolific, productive, and successful innovators. He famously said that innovation is one percent inspiration and 99 percent perspiration. His perspiration not only got late-nineteenth-century New York to accept the phonograph, but also the lightbulb, electricity, and many other innovations that still shape our lives. Traits like perseverance, but also social intelligence, even collective intelligence, distinguished Edison from similarly smart and creative people like de Martinville, who came up with very clever ideas, only to see them forgotten.

COINS

The creative ideas of the creator are taken up by small groups of innovative people in *Collaborative Innovation Networks*. These are groups of about two to fifteen intrinsically motivated people, who get together to create something new—not because they are paid to do so, but because they care about their cause. They assemble around a common vision, which they want to come true. They are innovators and trendsetters by conviction, and not because they want to fill their bank account. They are convinced that what they are up to is unbelievably cool and they want to carry their conviction to the rest of the world. COINs are nothing new; they have been around since historical times.

While Thomas Edison got all the credit for his inventions, in fact his greatest invention was the creation of Menlo Park, a research lab in New Jersey where he assembled other creative geniuses such as William Hammer, working on the development of the lightbulb; Charles Batchelor, Edison's loyal right-hand man and prolific inventor of telegraph systems; John Kruesi, the builder of many of Edison's designs; and dozens of others. Even Nikola Tesla, inventor of the AC electric system, spent time working at Menlo Park—a prototypical COIN if there ever was one, and well before the Internet age.

With the advent of modern telecommunications, in particular the Internet, COINs have sprouted up all around the globe. COINs are responsible for creations ranging from microfinancing institutions in the developing world, LEGO Mindstorms, and even the Internet itself. Little did the world know that a new epoch was about to start when Tim Berners-Lee and Robert Cailliau advertised their brand-new World Wide Web system over lunch at the 1991 ACM Hypertext conference in San Antonio, Texas. Their improvised lunch session raised interest among students and researchers from as far away as Helsinki to California, from Alaska to Australia, and this far-flung group began working together. And the rest, as the saying goes, is history.

CLNS

Once the cool idea has been turned into a product by the COIN, people in the COIN bring the product to their friends and family. In a two-way learning process, this extended group, the *Collaborative Learning Network*, learns the basics of the product from the COIN members, makes suggestions for improvements, and points out deficiencies of the initial prototype.

Almost from the beginning, Edison teamed up with other innovators. While the relationships were sometimes tumultuous, they almost always were productive. When young Edison came to Boston early in his career as an inventor, he immediately immersed himself in the community of other telegraph inventors, producers, and investors. He rented work space in the shop of Charles Williams, a leading telegraph producer. Later, as an aspiring entrepreneur in New York, Edison formed a partnership with Franklin Pope, another leading telegraph engineer. His mentors also introduced him to patent attorneys and other inventors—a Collaborative Learning Network that was crucial for Edison's future success.

CINS

Finally, the enthusiasm of the *Collaborative Interest Network* carries the final product over the tipping point and turns it into a real trend. In this final phase, commercial interests come into play. While a CLN includes at most a few hundred people, the CIN encompasses thousands or even millions of loyal users, virtually guaranteeing the success of the product.

Early on in his career, Edison collaborated with the leading telegraph companies. Western Union and Gold & Stock Telegraph Company became his main customers, carrying his innovations to the remotest corners of the United States and Europe. Even before that, as a teenage boy, Edison had shown a knack for socializing with journalists, which helped him to grow and cultivate his celebrity status in the press. Having the press on his side was highly advantageous for fostering societal acceptance of his more disruptive innovations such as the phonograph. And so another crucial difference between Eduard-Leon Scott de Martinville and Edison was this: Edison showed himself a genius in building up a Collaborative Interest Network to carry his inventions over the tipping point.

Finding the Trendsetters

Now imagine how cool it would be if we were able to recognize the next Thomas Alva Edison while he was still a boy. Or if we could have predicted the success of the phonograph right at the time of its inception and recognized the failure of de Martinville's phonautograph. The good news is that this COIN-based innovation process can indeed be recognized and tracked from the outside. We can take a general understanding of how new trends develop and apply it to coolhunting, finding the next big thing. The trick is not to look for the trend, but to look for the Edisons, the cool people creating the cool trends.

Coolhunting means finding trends by finding the trendsetters. It means being on the lookout for the four-step process involving

(1) creator, (2) COIN, (3) CLN, and (4) CIN. The earlier in the process you can identify the trendsetters, the better. By the time new trends are being pushed by Collaborative Interest Networks, they have become pretty self-evident to the rest of the world. If you spot them in the Collaborative Learning Network phase, they are still somewhat under the radar, so you are ahead of the crowd. Finding the original creators, while they are still on their own, not yet supported by their surrounding COIN, is pretty hard. Who could have distinguished young Thomas Alva Edison from young Eduard-Leon Scott de Martinville? Both were aspiring young innovators. One went on to change the world, the other sank into oblivion. One succeeded in rallying a COIN, the other stayed a lone inventor. The best point

FIGURE 1–1. Hunting for buffalo is like hunting for cool trends—looking for tracks and following the swarm.

in time to find new emerging trends therefore is to look for the COINs. Once you have found the COINs, you have also found the new trends they are about to create. Now, how does this work?

Think back to our forebears. As depicted in Figure 1–1, man once hunted for prey on the prairies, trying to find a wild buffalo, whose meat would carry them through the winter. Coolhunting means hunting for your own buffalo in the Internet age. The parallels

FIGURE 1–2.
Coolfarming is like traditional farming, but instead of killing the prey, put it to productive use.

between the early hunter and the coolhunter in the Internet age are striking. The most successful early hunters had to read the mind of their prey; successful Internet coolhunters have to read the mind of their customers. Internet customers do not leave hoofprints and dung behind, but they leave traces nonetheless, in online bulletin boards and forums, in blogs, websites, and wikis. These virtual traces provide a similarly clear image to the well-informed coolhunter.

Once you have found your cool thing, it is up to you to help make it succeed. Think again back to our forebears hunting a buffalo. Once they caught and slaughtered their prey, it provided food for a fixed period of time only. Think of how much better it would be to catch the buffalo alive, tame it, and use it to pull a plow (like in Figure 1–2), or to breed and grow young buffalos as a never-ending source of milk and meat. This book tells you how to tame and grow your own buffalo herd in the process we call "coolfarming."

Growing Your Own Trends

Making cool trends happen means creating an environment where COINs flourish. Nurturing COINs is similar to nurturing a swarm of bees, such that the bees produce more honey or the swarm splits so that a new swarm will emerge. Organizations that want to nurture cool trends are like beekeepers supportive of swarming. Bee swarming is risky; it is hardly controllable, and yet, the expert beekeeper observing his hive will usually catch the swarm and get it back to double the honey output. The same metaphor applies to organizations supportive of COINs. Observe the COIN members, help them develop their ideas, provide a fertile nurturing ground for developing new ideas, and they will get their cool trends off the ground. Coolfarming is "making the COINs happen"—and it will be one of the key success factors for organizations and businesses of the future.

This book includes many examples, from biology, history, and recent business cases. We start with a detailed description of how bees coolhunt for the perfect location for a new hive, and how their building the new hive serves as a blueprint for human coolfarmers. Later we discuss how LEGO tapped into the collective intelligence of its Mindstorms hacker community, converting them into a swarm of dedicated coolfarmers who now do a tremendous job developing Mindstorms products—for free. We also explore how an open-source beer recipe helped a small brewery in Denmark build a global community of beer lovers who began growing their own business in return. We study how the MIT Media Lab OLPC (One Laptop Per Child) has become a serious threat to the Microsoft-Intel monopoly in the netbook laptop market, all in less than five years. We also look at how the largest Swiss retailer, Migros, launched a highly successful low-cost but high-quality product line called M-Budget by cannibalizing its own business.

Obviously, in the short term, managers can survive very well by keeping everything under control. But as soon as the next crisis strikes, hierarchically managed organizations have a much harder time coping with changes than self-organizing organizations do. Just like individual bees, which independently act for the benefit of the swarm,

members of self-organizing organizations will work without centralized command for the advantage of their group. My advice therefore
is: "Practice coolfarming while you still have time!" More and more
companies are willing to delegate power "to the edge" and empower
employees and customers to make far-reaching decisions. For example, Procter & Gamble outsources its coolhunting to its technology
entrepreneurs. They are rank-and-file P&G employees who—in their
spare time—spot cool new products and trends for their employer, be
it on supermarket shelves in Japan or in small bakeries in Italy.

Coolfarming Is More Than Managing a Project

Compared to conventional project management, coolfarming is a
very different process. In the past, well-run projects were centrally
managed, with a single project manager running the show, oversee-
ing everything. Coolfarming, on the other hand, is a decentralized
self-organizing process where each member of the COIN knows
what he has to do. But the difference between the two approaches is
not as radical as it seems. In fact, highly successful projects of the past
have been coolfarmed, with the project manager acting more like a
creator and coolfarmer than a dictator. In such projects, team members assume personal responsibility, they self-organize in the case of
sudden change, and they share the vision and goals of the team
leader. However, most of the time, daily life in a conventionally managed project looks quite different, resembling more a dictatorship
than a democracy.

Figure 1–3 illustrates the conventional project management
process. In a conventional project started by a conventional organization, the problem owner, usually a senior manager, first defines the
problem that the project will solve. She then pulls together a team of
people to brainstorm solutions. Once she has decided what solution
to choose, she picks a team leader, defines project milestones, and

decides on the desired final outcome of the project. Afterward, a project manager is appointed to take over project responsibility. His job is to run the project, following the original project plan as closely as possible. During execution of the project, the problem owner will

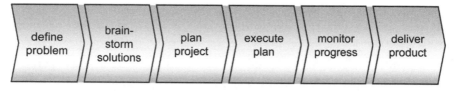

FIGURE 1–3. Conventional project management.

monitor progress and intervene if she decides that the project does not follow the plan anymore. In the end, the project team delivers the end product to the problem owner.

The coolfarming process, as shown in Figure 1–4, is entirely different. It starts with the fact that there is no problem owner. There is one person, the creator, who has an idea. In fact, she thinks the idea is so cool that, in spite of all obstacles, she wants to make it come true. She talks to many other people about her cool idea until, after many discussions, the creator finds a few people who agree to help. They latch on to the idea and in their spare time become a team—a Collaborative Innovation Network, or COIN—and they build a first, improvised version of the product.

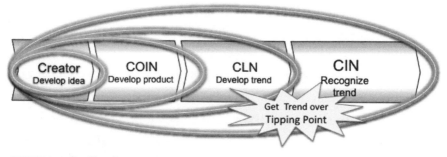

FIGURE 1–4. Coolfarming process.

The COIN members take their labor of love to their friends and family, continuously selling their idea to them. Using this group as a sounding board, the COIN collects feedback, improving the product, testing it out, and occasionally winning over a few select members to join the COIN. This group acts as the Collaborative Learning Network, or CLN, providing a reservoir of new COIN members, as well as external evangelists who help to get the product over the tipping point and convert it into a real trend. Once the new product has outgrown the word-of-mouth stage and is spoken about in mainstream media and admired by large groups of people, it will be embraced by the Collaborative Interest Network, or CIN. This is the commercialization phase of the trend, as CIN members spend real money to buy the product that they consider the pinnacle of cool. In this phase, the product makes it over the tipping point. It is no longer an "insider product" that is only known to a close-knit community of insiders and early followers; by now it has been turned into a real trend.

Let's look at the differences between conventional project management and coolfarming in more detail. As a first hypothetical example, let's compare how a new bike might be developed either as a conventionally managed project or, alternatively, through coolfarming.

In traditional project management, the owner of the project first defines the goals for the project. Let's assume Stella, the CEO of bike manufacturer TopBike, decides to develop a new type of mountain bike. She brainstorms possible solutions with some people close to her. She invites some of her factory's most loyal customers, together with the head of new product development and a few other engineers from TopBike, to a planning workshop, where they brainstorm the features their new bike will need to really stand out from the competition and continue to fuel the growth that the company has been experiencing so far. In this brainstorming workshop, the new product development team decides that the new bike needs to be much lighter and have a radically new gearshift mechanism.

Next, Stella pulls together a team to systematically plan, develop, and build the new bike. The head of new product development is tasked with coming up with a detailed plan in which the design of the new bike will be completed in eight months and will be available on the market in another four months. The engineers then start working together for the next eight months, indeed developing a bike that weighs 20 percent less than competing bikes and is equipped with a radically new and much more robust gearshift mechanism.

Once the bike is finished, TopBike's marketing people take over, launching a marketing blitz aimed at mountain bike journals and websites, touting the superior capabilities of the new bike. They also equip the mountain bike racing team they sponsor with the new bike, thus demonstrating the superior capabilities of the bike. This well-managed process is designed to eventually ensure solid sales and revenue growth for the next years at TopBike.

Now imagine how the same process would work in a coolfarming environment. There is no CEO to start the project, but there is Walter, a mechanical engineer at aircraft maker Boeing. Walter is a mountain biker fanatic who has climbed all the mountains around Seattle on his bike. Because he likes to test his bike's limits, as well as his own, and because he also competes in mountain biking races, he continuously tinkers with his bike. In particular, he thinks his bike is still far too heavy. Also, more than once, he barely avoided an accident in rough terrain when the gearshift suddenly got stuck. He talks with his colleagues at Boeing about his need for a lighter and still extremely stable and stiff bike frame. One of his friends at work suggests that he try out the new composite material they are using at Boeing for the aircraft wings.

Together with two of his best mountain biking buddies, Walter spends a few weekends in the aircraft factory, experimenting with the same composite material, until he succeeds in putting together a bike frame that weighs 50 percent less than all the commercially available bike frames yet is still extremely robust. For the gearshift, Walter taps into the collective intelligence of the mountain bikers hanging out in online communities at websites like Ning.com. He posts his request for a better gearshift on a couple of online forums that he regularly frequents. And indeed, he gets excellent advice from some other technically inclined Spanish mountain bikers in the Pyrenees, as well as from some bikers in the Appalachians. Exchanging ideas online, they come up with a simple but sturdy solution that has significantly less moving parts than existing commercially available gearshifts.

From inception to having a first prototype of his lightweight bike with sturdy gearshift took Walter about twelve months. It was a nonlinear process, hitting a few roadblocks along the way, which Walter was able to overcome thanks to his good social network at Boeing. His new bike attracts the attention of other bikers, particularly when he successfully competes in some local mountain bike races. As he shares his insights about his radically new design with other bikers, word-of-mouth spreads, both online, in the mountain biking forums, and through envious onlookers on the trail. Soon, other bikers start copying his design, and some other, less mechanically gifted bikers ask him if he will manufacture one for them too. Walter starts producing a small batch of his newly designed bike, continuously tinkering with the design, and adding more small improvements. His first series sells out quickly, and orders start streaming in over the Internet. As he cannot handle the increasing workload all by himself, he asks some of the colleagues in his mountain biking club for help. Together they start a small company. The company grows quickly and the business expands rapidly, first regionally, but soon after on a national level, and then, within their first business year, also on an international level.

Walter is an archetype of a successful coolfarmer and creator, who first forms a COIN with his closest biking buddies, then extends it to a CLN by integrating feedback from early adopters of his product, and finally grows it into a global CIN of loyal customers.

The basic principle of coolfarming is to not directly invite others in, but to advertise the idea and let others find the group and the idea. They will come because the idea appeals to them, and because they respect the flag bearers. This means that the community initially will grow at a slower rate, but it will be more sustainable and much less susceptible to problems, such as strong egos, that can hold back success of the team. A coolfarming team also won't allow messenger-killers and pontificators, as the group will police them whenever they try to rise up, kicking them out if need be.

The risk that the group will fall prey to groupthink is much smaller than in conventional teams, because a coolfarming COIN has a culture of constructive criticism as a central part of its group DNA. Since the group is extremely focused on a shared vision, it will police off-topic time-wasters. An organically growing COIN will be extremely efficient in processing and unifying diverse levels of understanding to develop a shared understanding and vocabulary. This means that the group will communicate at a much deeper level of understanding than a superficially cobbled-together project team.

As the comparison in Table 1–1 indicates, the emphasis for conventional project management is on planning, execution, and monitoring, while the focus of coolfarming is on self-motivation, self-organization, and peer recognition. This does not mean that coolfarmers expect to work for free forever. Rather, they are risk takers who are convinced of the potential of a new idea or concept, and they are willing to invest their own resources, be it time, social capital, or money, in the new idea without knowing yet how they'll be paid back for their investment. If they are right in their assessment, they will be paid back in the end, perhaps through increased reputation or through financial rewards, or a combination of both. But like good bees, they will keep the interests of the swarm ahead of their own, knowing that if the swarm does well, so will they.

TABLE 1–1. **Comparing project management and coolfarming.**

	Project Management	Coolfarming
Motivation	Extrinsic	Intrinsic
Management style	Supervised	Self-organized
Innovation type	Planned innovation	Disruptive innovation
Measuring project progress	Fixed milestones	Dynamic development

Let's now look at two famous examples of highly successful coolfarming—the World Wide Web and Linux.

Coolfarming the World Wide Web

When Tim Berners-Lee first introduced his hypertext system, little did he know that his system would change the world.

In his original vision, Tim described a system that would finally implement the architecture first described by Vannevar Bush, long-time president of MIT and wartime scientific adviser to President Franklin Roosevelt during World War II. In his famous article, "As We May Think," published in the *Atlantic Monthly* in July 1945, Bush described a system in which microfiche viewers would put at the reader's fingertips all the knowledge of mankind. He also envisioned some mechanical implementation of hyperlinking, where the reader could click on some highlighted piece of information to call up another document. Over the next forty years Bush's ideas were picked up by many researchers, most famously Ted Nelson, who coined the term *hypertext*, and Douglas Engelbart, who invented the computer mouse, thus enabling us to mouse-click on a link in a web document.

In the early 1990s, there was an entire branch of computer science dedicated to hypertext, the science of linking different pieces of information. It was at the annual gathering of this research community that Tim presented his ideas. As a young post-doctoral researcher at MIT back then, I was part of this research community and thus also present at the 1991 ACM Hypertext conference in San Antonio when Tim described his system. Somehow, we had all missed the point. We were too much enamored of elegant ideas and concepts and did not care enough about end-users outside the academic ivory tower to bother to get our hypertext systems into the hands of everyday people. It took Tim, the IT consultant from the United Kingdom, working in a physics research lab (CERN) in Switzerland, to teach us how to do it. The archetypical creator, if there ever was one, Tim Berners-Lee did not care about status and prestige for himself, but only about his ideas. He succeeded where hundreds of academics with PhDs from the most prestigious universities had failed.

I vividly remember Tim passing out handouts during the conference. He had no official conference paper about the new system he was proposing, which he called the "World Wide Web," but equipped with a pile of flyers, he pressed one into the hand of anybody he was able to talk to. In the flyer, he and his colleague, Robert Cailliau, also from CERN, described their system. They also offered a prototype version of the very first web server and web browser for free download from their server at CERN. Tim organized a session during lunch in San Antonio, where he got enough people excited enough to form a small group to further develop his vision. While we academics had been presenting scientific concepts, Tim was presenting a workable vision. Although he had very little money, he put his full energy and personality behind his vision to attract similarly minded people—as befits a creator—and thus had a way to get this idea off the ground.

One of the people attending that lunch session was Dan Connolly, a recent computer science graduate from the University of Texas at Austin. Another was Pei-Yuan Wei, a student at the University of California, Berkeley, who developed the Viola browser, the first popular browser for the Web. Tim, Robert, Pei-Yuan, Dan, and a few others formed one of the first true COINs. This Collaborative Innovation Network was absolutely critical in turning the vision of the Web into a real product.

Almost singlehandedly, Tim and Robert had developed a first prototype of the Web, but it was clumsy and would only run on Unix Next workstations, which were somewhat popular at universities, but practically nonexistent outside academia. They needed the help of their fellow COIN members to take the Web to the next step, developing and immediately publishing new releases of web servers and browsers on more popular computer platforms. Putting his passion before everything else, Tim chose to work at MIT so that he could further develop the Web.

Tim came to MIT as a visiting scientist, hosted by the group where I worked. Initially, he had no official office and worked from a small desk in the hallway. This did not distract him in the least from further pushing and developing his system. He was constantly communicating with the initial members of his COIN, circulating proposals for extending the Web and trying to recruit new COIN members. Michael Dertouzos, director of the MIT Laboratory for Computer Science at that time, was an early and unwavering supporter of the

Web and succeeded in establishing the World Wide Web Consortium (W3C) with Tim a little more than a year later.

In 1994, the first World Wide Web conference was held at CERN. I had returned to Switzerland one year earlier and started working for UBS, the largest Swiss bank, as a manager in the software development department. When I learned about the conference, I tried to register, but I was told that the conference was already heavily oversubscribed and totally sold out. The Collaborative Learning Network (CLN) had taken over, providing a vibrant and rapidly growing nurturing ground to spawn more COINs developing different flavors of web servers and browsers. When I participated in the World Wide Web conference in Darmstadt, Germany, the subsequent year—I had learned my lesson and registered well in advance—the enthusiasm was unbelievable. The audience was still mostly academic, but the first businesses had latched onto the idea and were present as well. Large vendors like Apple and Sun Microsystems, plus dozens of smaller vendors, were showcasing first versions of their web-based products. The Web was now close to reaching its tipping point.

I was still working for UBS and was suggesting to my bosses that we build one of the first corporate Intranets—we called it the "Bank Wide Web"—of course based on web technology. But my bosses insisted on using a "more robust, commercially supported" product called Oracle Card, from database vendor Oracle. With senior UBS staff members, we built an Oracle Card–based version of the "Bank Wide Web" while I recruited two summer interns from MIT to build a web-based version of this application on a shoestring budget. Only when my boss went to the annual Gartner Group conference and heard the analysts singing the praises of the World Wide Web did he allow me to switch the "official" Bank Wide Web to run on an open-source web server. Now the Collaborative Interest Network

(CIN) had taken over, and monetary interests were driving further development of the Web.

A year earlier, Marc Andreessen, then a student at the National Center for Supercomputing Applications (NCSA) at the University of Illinois at Urbana-Champaign, had released the first version of an easy-to-use web browser called Mosaic, which for the first time displayed pictures right inside the browser. For our web-based Bank Wide Web at UBS, we used Mosaic. Later, when Andreessen had left NCSA and started Netscape Communications (together with serial entrepreneur and former Stanford professor Jim Clark), we immediately switched to the commercially supported Netscape browser. When, as a UBS manager, I visited Netscape Communications in 1995 in their start-up offices in Palo Alto, it was a bustling company, growing so rapidly that it had no time to send me an invoice for the Netscape licenses we were using at UBS. The Web had now definitively reached its tipping point, and the Collaborative Interest Network had done a stellar job of turning this innovation into one hell of a trend!

Coolfarming Linux

The way the Linux operation system evolved to become a major alternative to Microsoft is another excellent example of coolfarming. In 1991, Finnish computer science student Linus Torvalds invited other computer freaks to download, test, and extend his "free operating system, just a hobby . . ." (quoted from Linus's original e-mail). At that time Unix, the predecessor of Linux, was already looking back on a long and successful history. Unix was created by Ken Thompson and Dennis Ritchie, two researchers at the world-famous Bell Labs in the late sixties and early seventies, and had been quickly embraced by the academic community. It was the platform of choice of computer science students and was further developed by the University of

California, Berkeley, among others. Companies like Sun and Silicon Graphics also had built entire businesses on top of it.

When I was a student at the University of Zurich in the mid-1980s, all of our computer science classes were using Unix minicomputers. Personal computers from companies like Atari or Apple were just emerging, IBM had not yet launched its PC. When the IBM PC and its clones appeared, Unix got another boost, as computer science professors started porting versions of Unix to the PC. This way, for the first time, computer science students could get their own hands dirty tinkering with operating systems.

Operating systems are hugely complex beasts that the end-user normally does not want to touch. In the old days of huge water-cooled mainframe computers from IBM, only the computer operator in his white lab overcoat was allowed to touch the operating system. In my computer classes in the mid-eighties, we were using so-called minicomputers running Unix from computer manufacturer Digital Equipment Corporation (DEC) instead of huge mainframes, but these computers were still enviously guarded by operators, and students were only allowed to use them a few hours a day to run their own programs. For my own computer science PhD thesis at the University of Zurich, I mostly had to simulate my new ideas outside of the existing operating system, as we were not allowed to directly modify the source code of the Unix operating system at one of the precious minicomputers.

All this changed with the availability of the IBM PC and its clones, and some computer science professors started rewriting simple versions of Unix for teaching purposes for the PC. One of the most widely used of these new versions of Unix was Minix, a Unix clone developed by computer science professor Andrew Tanenbaum at Vrije Universiteit in Amsterdam. By 1991, different versions of Unix were widely available and heavily used by academics and researchers, but they were still leading somewhat of a niche life in the business world, where IBM mainframes and DEC minicomputers dominated.

While the different versions of Unix were accessible to academics, they were still only mostly accessible as executable "binary" code, not as source code, which could easily be modified and recompiled into binary form for redistribution. The notable exception was the Berkeley Software Distribution, the so-called BSD Unix. But even the rights to this distribution were jealously guarded by Berkeley until another academic of legendary reputation as a computer hacker set out to change matters.

Richard Stallman, a programmer at the MIT Lab for Computer Science, started a project called GNU—short for "GNU's not Unix"—with the goal of creating a "new Unix" that wasn't based on the protected versions owned by Bell Labs and Berkeley. Stallman is a stereotypical computer nerd, with long hair and awe-inspiring programming skills. At one point, Stallman spent so much time behind the keyboard that, thanks to carpal tunnel syndrome, his hands grew totally numb and he could not use a keyboard anymore. He therefore had to hire MIT undergraduate students and dictate his computer programs to them, similar to how an executive might dictate a letter to the secretary. Because he wanted to make his computer programs accessible to all, Stallman started the Free Software Foundation, whose goal it was to make its software available to everybody in source-code format. Users of free software have the obligation to provide for free to the rest of the world all changes they might make to a piece of free software. In 1991, Stallman had been hard at work for almost a decade, singlehandedly recreating large parts of Unix, although failing in his ultimate goal of recreating a fully functional version of the operating system.

This task fell to Linus Torvalds. As a young student from Finland he was quite an unlikely candidate to assume the role of creator of the only real contender to Microsoft's operating system, which dominated the small server market. In 1991 Torvalds was studying computer science in Helsinki and experimenting with Andrew Tanenbaum's Minix, trying to create a ". . . free operating system (just a hobby, won't be big and professional like GNU). . . ." Well, it turned out that his hobby, Linux, would become much bigger and more professional than GNU, thanks mostly to his superb coolfarming skills as a creator. As soon as Torvalds had finished the first halfway-working version of his new operating system, he widely announced it on the Internet, at the same time inviting everybody to change and extend it. The only request he had was that any extensions to his system be made available for reintegration into his original product. But unlike Richard Stallman, he did not forbid other users from making money by selling an extended version of Linux.

As a creator, Torvalds is a terrific role model. His personality is very different from both Andrew Tanenbaum, Minix's author, and Richard Stallman, the driving force behind GNU. Unlike Tanenbaum, who had written all of Minix by himself, even asserting his ownership in a publicized e-mail exchange with Torvalds, Linus invited other people from day one to extend and modify his brainchild. He never claimed to be the smartest person in the room; rather, he was challenging others to come up with solutions better than his own.

Torvalds also strongly differs from Stallman, who, with religious zeal, insists on the free aspect of software. GNU's modifications need to be given back to the community, for free. Torvalds has a much more relaxed and far less religious attitude. Linux and Linux extensions may be sold commercially. As it turned out, these were crucial differences. This openness to the ideas of others, in combination with a more relaxed attitude toward commercialization, made Linux a quick favorite among all open-source operating systems. The feedback Torvalds received to his first post was overwhelming, and less than six months after the initial announcement, the first Linux online newsgroup was founded.

The success of Linux is all the more amazing when you consider that unlike Tim Berners-Lee, Torvalds had no famous research organizations, such as CERN or MIT, to use as a springboard. And while Tim Berners-Lee worked on a shoestring budget, at least he had a budget. For the first years of development, Linux was entirely dependent on free labor. Also, while the World Wide Web Consortium is now hosted by MIT, Linux, even today, has no official organizational home other than the computer of Linus Torvalds.

But Torvalds is a master of motivating people. In his first messages, he did a superb job of appealing to the ego of programmers, successfully recruiting other top developers. Within the first six to twelve months he successfully formed his COIN, attracting people like Ari Lemmke, who suggested the name Linux and started the main online newsgroup for Linux. Alan Cox, a Welsh programmer, became a trusted lieutenant to Linus Torvalds. Ted Ts'o, initially an MIT student and later an MIT employee, who in 1991 became the first Linux kernel programmer from North America, added the initial networking functionality, together with Alan Cox.

While collaborating to rapidly develop Linux, the initial COIN members started growing their community and forming a Collaborative Learning Network. Spreading the news about the capabilities of Linux, they mostly used word-of-mouth propaganda on the Internet, quickly establishing a devoted group of followers. I remember how, in early 1996, I had to recompile the Linux system on my IBM PC at home to get it to recognize my particular hardware configuration. This work wasn't for the fainthearted, as it required pretty substantial computer science skills. But, according to Torvalds, this was precisely what early Linux users were looking for. After all, he advertised Linux with the following words: "[W]hen men were men and wrote their own device drivers . . . [they were] just dying to cut their teeth on an operating system they can try to modify for their needs."

The very first so-called "Linux distribution," a bundled set of software to make installation easier, was published in November 1992, followed by many others. Each of these distributions formed its own Collaborative Learning Network of software developers compiling the distribution and catering to the needs of a much larger group of dedicated users of the particular Linux distribution. The three most famous of these distributions, Debian, Slackware, and Ubuntu, each regularly launched new versions of their software, with some of the technically more ambitious users shifting over time from being consumers to members of the core distribution team, a COIN of dedicated Linux programmers.

When Red Hat started to sell its first commercial software distribution in 1995, Linux definitively turned the corner. It was no longer a hobby of computer aficionados but a mainstream business. Red Hat was followed by other vendors of commercial Linux distributions, with the goal of making installation of Linux as simple for the end-user as installation of Windows. A Collaborative Interest Network (CIN) quickly sprang up, made up of users of Red Hat Linux and SUSE, the other leading commercial Linux distribution (which was acquired in 2003 by Novell). At the same time, industry heavyweights IBM and HP started generating billions of dollars of Linux-based revenue. In 1997, when the Slashdot online forum was launched as one of the main virtual hangouts of tech geeks, it quickly became the main platform for sharing the latest Linux rumors among members of the Linux CIN.

Today, Linux is well established as the leading operating system for web servers, as well as an operating system for personal computers sold by Dell, HP, and IBM. According to IDC,[2] revenue generated through selling Linux software will cross $1 billion in 2012. This in addition to the much higher revenue generated through selling Linux-based hardware and consulting services by companies such as IBM, HP, and Dell. Quite astounding for an operating system that was started as a hobby by a student seventeen years ago. This is coolfarming at its best!

Table 1–2 chronicles the four steps—"creator-COIN-CLN-CIN"—for both the creation of the World Wide Web and the creation of Linux.

As we have seen, Tim Berners-Lee and Linus Torvalds are the very best kind of role models for coolfarmers. Coolfarmers care about the idea first. If they do it right, financial rewards and other success will

Table 1-2. Coolfarming the World Wide Web and Linux.

	World Wide Web	Linux
Creator (innovate) **Develop concept** **Evangelize**	Tim Berners-Lee creates WWW concept; introduces it at Hypertext '91 conference	Linus Torvalds writes 1st Linux kernel; sends e-mail invitation to Minix newsgroup
COIN (collaborate) **Develop product** **Evangelize**	Student group develops HTML/ HTTP; evangelizes through WWW Consortium	Student group develops Linux kernel
CLN (communicate) **Develop trend** **Evangelize**	Early adopters set up web servers at universities/companies; promote at WWW conferences	Debian distribution developers/early adopters compile Linux at home/universities/companies
CIN (communicate/share interest) **Use/buy product**	Organizations widely deploy web servers; Netscape commercializes/makes Web usable for everybody	SUSE/Red Hat started; end-users widely deploy Linux; Slashdot started

TIME

come later on! We will study how precisely they do it in the chapter about creators. But before we do that, let's have a closer look at the engine enabling all this great coolfarming: swarm creativity, the main force behind the power of collaborative innovation. How precisely does it work?

2

Swarm Creativity
The Force That Fuels Coolfarming

The volunteers are deeply committed to making the best translation, and they don't care how long it takes them. . . . There is a passion there that you don't get from hired guns.

June Cohen, Executive producer TED Media,
on the quality of volunteer translators*

NOTHING BEATS THE creativity of devoted swarms. While many groundbreaking ideas have been invented by smart and dedicated individuals, none of these individuals would have been successful without the support of a dedicated swarm. It is not the individual inventor tinkering away in his garage or even in a large corporate research laboratory, but the collective efforts of groups of people that get the next great idea off the ground. Examples in today's Internet economy abound, as we have just seen in the creation and further development

* "A Web That Speaks Your Language," http://www.nytimes.com, May 17, 2009

of the World Wide Web and open-source computer programs like Linux. Commercial companies such as Procter & Gamble, LEGO, and Google also are thriving based on the same principles.

Members of these groups of idea creators work long hours, delivering amazing results—motivated only by their love of the idea itself and by their feeling of being part of a team that can change the world. They set out initially not with thoughts of realizing financial gain, but rather with hopes of meeting a challenge or solving a puzzle and, in doing so, making the world a better place. In the case of commercial companies, as convincingly demonstrated by P&G, LEGO, and Google, in due time they also achieve stellar returns.

The people in these groups are not only creative, but swarm creative. "Swarm creativity" describes the positive behavior that results in the kind of collective mindset that generates such outstanding results. In biology, the term *swarm* is used to describe the behavior of a group of animals traveling in the same direction. The swarming of bees exemplifies this concept. Without central direction, bees self-organize to build nests, feed and grow their offspring, gather food, and even decide who becomes their next queen. Humans traveling together in the same creative, innovative direction produce the most interesting and exciting trends. The swarm creativity unleashed by groups of humans swarming together beats any creativity organized on demand.

With the tremendous expansion of online communication, the ability of humans to engage in swarm creativity has grown exponentially. Creative swarms can form instantaneously and collaborate on innovative tasks from almost anywhere on the planet, crossing all organizational boundaries. In companies large and small, groups of creative individuals swarm together to explore ideas about which they care deeply, irrespective of any direct or immediate connection to the bottom line. These emergent nuclei of swarms are the Collaborative Innovation Networks, or COINs.

Our swarming model of COIN-based innovation is based on three principles. They are a logical consequence of using swarm creativity.

1. Gain power by giving it away. This is the most important principle. Give everyone involved in a Collaborative Innovation Network, no matter what their level of involvement, the feeling that they have come up with the new ideas, that they are part of the solution and invaluable contributors, so that all members feel a strong sense of ownership. This also means that it is perfectly fine, and accepted by the rest of the community, for any COIN member to walk away from the COIN at any point in time.

2. Mandate intrinsic motivation. This principle unleashes swarm creativity, and it ties in with giving power to the community, letting it self-organize while providing a nurturing ground for creative ideas to flower. This means in particular that, at least initially, COIN members should never be paid to be part of the COIN. Trends can be created with good ideas. Set an innovative idea free and share knowledge for free in a community or network. If the community accepts the new idea and the COIN begins to grow, the idea becomes a new trend. Community builders provide everything at their disposal to potential swarms to be creative, and then they let swarm creativity happen. In this sense, they "mandate" swarms into action to create something new. Financial incentives should not be part of this initial mix. They might come later, but at least at the start, they will only distract the COIN members from their goals.

3. To find the cool trends, find the cool people. Great coolfarmers are also great coolhunters—just think of venture capitalists. The best ones know that any great idea also takes a great team to get it off the ground, and it is these teams that VCs are looking for. When scouring the Web or hunting for the next cool thing, coolfarmers look for crystallization points, namely in the form of leaders who embed themselves in their networks, not as stars but as members of swarms. They then try to recruit these kinds of leaders to join their cause.

These three principles of swarm creativity are combined in "cool-farming." The objective is to get intrinsically motivated people on board early on, people who care more about the cause than about their egos. Ideally, they are well respected in their community and volunteer to become the "flag bearers" or "lighthouses." These people then get others to sign on. Just being an expert, or being famous, is not enough. What is at least as important is a high degree of "collective intelligence," to be described in detail in Chapter 8.

At this point it is worthwhile to look at the difference between "swarm creativity" and "swarm intelligence." These two terms get mixed up frequently. In particular, we need to distinguish between the terms "intelligence" and "creativity."

Intelligence means that we are able to understand and react in complex situations, that we interpret the meaning of something happening and are able to choose the best solution from different options. The term *swarm intelligence* was first coined by computer scientist Eric Bonabeau, who was inspired by social insects.[1] In particular, Bonabeau looked at the intelligence of ants, which are able to collectively find the shortest path to a food source by laying pheromone trails.

Creativity stands for something different. It means coming up with something fundamentally new, with original solutions to a problem, by applying concepts from different, seemingly unrelated fields to the chosen problem domain. It means thinking independently, "outside the box," applying one's own judgment to the problem unrestricted by common and popular opinion. As creators of large groups, social insects such as bees make excellent role models of swarm creativity. Bees show emergent patterns of swarm creativity, collectively creating new hives, choosing their new queen, and locating the best food sources.

Humans excel in jointly creating new and innovative things. In fact, it seems that all progress that mankind has made throughout history is due to swarm creativity. By his own words, only by "standing on the shoulders of giants" could Isaac Newton come up with his groundbreaking insights about gravity, building on what others before him had found out, ranging back to old Archimedes in ancient Greek times. The same is true for any especially creative human being. Leonardo da Vinci based his insights on ideas of Greek and Roman artists, philosophers, and mathematicians. Thomas Alva Edison had a long line of inventors, including Eduard-Leon Scott de Martinville, to draw upon when inventing the lightbulb and the phonograph. In fact, the more opportunities that humans have to network and interact, the more creative they become.

As evolutionary biologist Jared Diamond in his book *Gun, Germs, and Steel*[2] has convincingly shown, the Mediterranean region was the hotbed of civilization for the last 10,000 years only because it was such a crossroads of cultures and people at the intersection of Asia, northern Africa, and Europe. It was the sheer mass of people mixing and mingling that made it the most innovative region. Silk Road travelers from China, caravans of traders from Timbuktu, and Viking raiders from Norway all came together in the Mediterranean basin, exchanging knowledge and learning from each other. In other regions that were cut off from the Eurasian basin, such as Africa south of the Sahara, North and South America, and Australia, innovation progressed at a much slower pace, with the pace being roughly proportional to the size of the population interacting with each other. While Africans south of the Sahara still were able to independently discover uses for iron, this was not possible for the smaller groups of people in America or Australia. In fact, in the much smaller population in the highlands of Papua New Guinea, which neighbors Australia, tribes were still living in the Stone Age well into the twentieth century.

The simple point I would like to make is the following: The more opportunities we have to network and swarm together, the more creative we become. This is true not only for humans, but also for apes.

Although the term *creativity* is commonly reserved for humans, it occasionally is used with the great apes, too. For example, researchers observed chimpanzees using sticks to poke for termites (food) through holes in walls of baked clay too narrow to get through by hand. What researchers further found is that chimpanzees in smart company—that is, in groups with other creative chimpanzees—were more creative. While there were entire tribes of chimpanzees not using tools, there were others that often did use tools to access food, with young chimpanzees learning the tricks of the trade from their elders. So, swarm creativity also exists in chimpanzee land.

The More Swarms Communicate, the Better They Perform

My own Internet-age research projects, looking at software start-ups in Israel, found that the more company CEOs communicated with their peers, the higher their chances of business success.[3] To be more specific, my colleague Ornit Raz analyzed the communication network of the leaders of 100 software start-ups in Israel in 1998. We then checked which of the 100 companies were still around in 2005—that is, which companies had survived the bursting of the e-business bubble in 2001. It turned out that the more CEOs had communicated with their peers in 1998, the higher the chances that their companies were still around in 2005. The more CEOs spoke with their potential competitors, either in informal discussions or in formal alliances, the better their chances of surviving after the bubble burst. The more

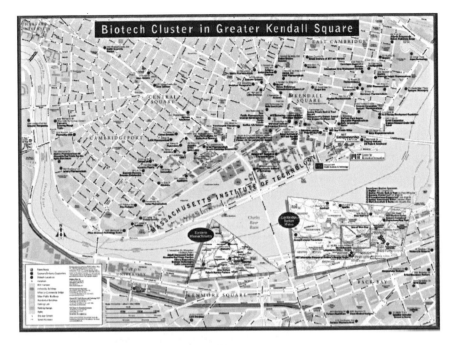

FIGURE 2–1. Map of the Boston Biotech Cluster. *Source: MIT Entrepreneurship Center.*

swarming among CEOs—even with the competition—the better their companies did!

In a second MIT project, my colleagues Tom Allen and Ornit Raz looked at the communication among research labs.[4] The Boston Biotech Cluster (see Figure 2–1) is a hotbed of medical innovation, consisting of roughly 500 companies, ranging from three-person start-ups to large publicly traded companies like Biogen Idec and Amgen. Scientists working at 150 of the biotech start-ups in the Boston cluster were asked for information about which scientists from other companies and research labs they communicated with. For an entire year, on a random day every week, the scientists reported the names of the companies and universities they had spoken with on that particular day.

The results were striking. First, the closer together the companies were in physical proximity, the more the scientists spoke with

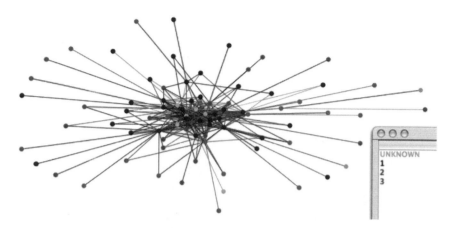

FIGURE 2–2. *The closer to the center, the more intense the communication. Black indicates less than two miles from center; dark gray, two to five miles from center; light gray, more than five miles from center. Note that the distance between dots (i.e., companies) shows intensity of communication, not location.*

scientists from the other companies (see Figure 2–2). Most communication happened within a five-mile radius around MIT and Harvard; companies more than five miles away showed a dramatic drop in communication activity. This was totally unexpected because—in the age of telecommunication—it is quite easy to contact anybody, anywhere, using the phone, e-mail, or other electronic means of communication. And yet, scientists communicated much more with scientists from other companies within a fifteen-minute driving distance. Also, the most active communication partners of the start-ups were not other start-ups, but, by a large margin, the two universities: MIT and Harvard. Note that the researchers at MIT and Harvard did not actively participate in the study; even so, MIT and Harvard were at the center of the communication because they were so frequently named by the start-up researchers.

The companies whose scientists spoke the most with their peers and competitors were the most productive in coming up with new ideas, measured by patent count. This means that the more scientists spoke with other researchers from competitors, the more creative they were. And, as we just have shown, they could better their chances of talking to their peers by getting closer together, and by getting closer to MIT and Harvard. Helping to form creative swarms is therefore good for the company, even if the members of the creative swarm come from other companies and outside research labs. And there are other advantages for companies that operate as swarms.

Swarm Business Beats "Black Swans"

Self-organizing swarms are much better in coping with catastrophic failures. While conventional wisdom, still touted by politicians and the military, teaches that hierarchical organization is more efficient in times of crisis, this is simply not always true. Too frequently, efficiency just means reaction speed. What if the decisive reaction taken by the few in the name of the many is the wrong one for the many?

In the fall of 2008, the financial world was thrown into turmoil. The demise of investment banks Lehman Brothers, Merrill Lynch, and Bear Stearns was only the tip of the iceberg. Unscrupulous dealings of investment bankers to optimize short-term profits had brought the financial system to its knees. From the outside, it looked as if Wall Street was hit by huge, external catastrophic events that nobody could have predicted in advance, just like 9/11, when a small group of terrorists suddenly attacked New York City's Twin Towers using hijacked airplanes. Only, these large unexpected events are bound to happen every so often, and turn upside down all our sophisticated prediction models.

In the Middle Ages, people believed that all swans had to be white, so a black swan could not possibly exist. In 2008, black swans struck the proud investment banks of Wall Street.

Nassim Nicholas Taleb wrote this about the banking industry in his best-selling 2007 book, *The Black Swan*: "The financial ecology is swelling into gigantic, incestuous, bureaucratic banks—when one falls, they all fall. The increased concentration among banks seems to have the effect of making financial crisis less likely, but when they happen they are more global in scale and hit us very hard. . . . We would be far better off if there were a different ecology, in which financial institutions went bust on occasion and were rapidly replaced by new ones." Taleb showed uncanny foresight only a year before the subprime mortgage crisis started pulling the largest banks down into the deepest crisis of their history. Citibank, UBS, and Bear Stearns supposedly had ironclad risk management, to avoid precisely the sort of financial meltdown they were experiencing in 2008. As Taleb writes, these banks are extremely good at planning for all sorts of foreseeable risks, only to be hit by the "big one," the black swan, the one devastating blow that nobody predicted.

Self-organizing swarms are much better at dealing with those sorts of catastrophes. Just look at the bees. In a swarm of bees, if some of the honey collectors are hit by accidents, the swarm continues functioning flawlessly. Even if a really big crisis hits the swarm, it copes extremely well. Take, for example, the unexpected death of the queen. In this case bees will immediately and autonomously engage in succession planning. They will choose an ordinary larva and start feeding it royal jelly, which will turn it into a queen. They do this without central intervention; rather, they act by a self-organizing decision of the swarm. This way the swarm evades extinction and quickly gets a new egg-laying queen, ensuring further prosperity of the swarm.

The same is true for a swarm business. In an article written for *Sloan Management Review*,[5] I defined a "swarm business" as a business operating on the principles of swarm creativity and COINs, with a focus on the swarm first and making money second. In such a decentralized self-organizing business, risk management is not a highly centralized function, directly reporting to an imperial CEO, but is part of everybody's daily job. In a swarm business, there will continuously be minor glitches and small catastrophes, but it will not be possible to have the kind of catastrophic meltdowns the financial markets were experiencing in 2008.

The Internet already gives us a model of this decentralized financial model. For more than ten years, eBay has been considered one of the poster children of the Internet economy by providing an online marketplace for everything. At first glance, eBay very much looks like a swarm business. By empowering many small traders to start their own businesses, it has created an ecosystem of stakeholders selling their specialized wares on the eBay platform. The company takes a cut from everything that is being sold on its website. The reason this works, and people are willing to pay a fraction of the sales price to eBay, is that it acts as an intermediary of trust, guaranteeing the flow of money from the buyer to the vendor. In this sense, eBay holds a central position in its ecosystem.

Compare eBay with Craigslist, where everybody can post things to sell or buy for free, without the need for a central intermediary and, for the most part, without having to pay a fee. In this regard, Craigslist[6] is actually a far better model for a swarm business than eBay. It is the swarm, the buyers of goods on Craigslist, who are responsible for ensuring trust, which they do by policing each other and reporting abuse on Craigslist to each other and to the operators of Craigslist. As Craig Newmark, founder and chairman of Craigslist, says: "Helping people out by doing some good has worked pretty well for us." Although Craig lives by his self-proclaimed "nerd values" and claims that there is nothing altruistic about his company, his principles clearly are to the advantage of the swarm. He also describes Craigslist as a community-meta-organizer, again emphasizing the swarm business foundations of his company.

"Creative swarming" is highly beneficial for individuals and companies alike. It is the best way of coming up with cool new ideas. As groups of people, we are coolfarmers of new ideas, reusing old ideas, combining them, and converting them into new ones. The question now is: What do these basic insights in swarm creativity mean for coolfarmers? To take a first deep-dive into the inner workings of creative swarms, let's leave the human coolfarmers for a moment and look again at the bees, those intrinsically motivated coolfarmers in the animal kingdom.

Lessons from the Beehive

Swarms of bees are unbelievably successful at coolhunting and coolfarming. A bee hunting for honey is like a human coolhunter. While the human coolhunter is hunting for the latest cool trends, the bee coolhunter is hunting for honey. The parallel also applies to coolfarming. A bee doing her waggle dance to recruit other bees to her honey source corresponds to the coolfarming members of a COIN recruiting other people to join their cause. So let's look at what human coolfarmers can learn from the way bees do their coolhunting and coolfarming.

Bees are exemplars of self-organization, accomplishing the most complex tasks seemingly without central coordination. Bees build perfectly shaped hexagonal honeycombs without any obvious leaders. They raise their brood in perfect communal sharing. The swarm decides who will become the new queen; the old queen does not, as one might expect, make this decision through laying a special egg. Their self-organizing system to allocate resources to honey collection through waggle dancing is so effective that operators of web server farms have started copying it. In a waggle dance, a bee, which has found a promising honey source, starts "dancing" in the hive, with other bees joining her dance. Her dance tells the other bees where to find the honey source. The more excited the first waggle dancer is, the more other bees will join the dance and subsequently start flying to the same honey source. In fact, it makes more sense to look at the entire swarm of bees as one immortal superorganism rather than focusing on the individual bee. The way that bees swarm—creating a superorganism—can be a blueprint for the "creator-COIN-CLN-CIN" process. While a swarm of bees splits and replicates to carry on and improve its gene pool, the members of COINs grow in number and split as carriers of new ideas and trends.

Figure 2–3 illustrates the four-step coolfarming process for honeybees. The creator of a new swarm is the queen bee, setting out to create a new hive. Once the swarm has left the hive by following the queen, it first temporarily settles on a branch, clustered around the queen (Figure 2–4). The swarm then sends out scouts to hunt for a permanent location for the hive. These bee scouts are the equivalent

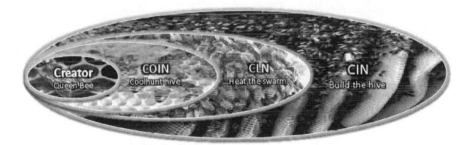

FIGURE 2–3. How swarming bees do their coolfarming.

of the COIN members and coolhunters. They need to convince their sisters back in the swarm of the merits of the new location for the swarm. First, they individually try to influence their sisters through active waggle dancing. The bee whose waggle dance is the most convincing will slowly but steadily grow her following. Other bees will pick up her waggle dancing and pass on the location to other waggle dancers. This gradually growing group of coolhunters corresponds to the Collaborative Learning Network (CLN), where new members

FIGURE 2–4. Swarming bees.

join the original COIN by learning the tricks of the trade—or the location of the new hive—from the core COIN members.

Once enough bees in the swarm accept the merits of the new hive location, the swarm literally explodes, which means it gets over the tipping point. This explosion is triggered by the coolhunting bees, the CLN and COIN members beeping at other bees, climbing from one bee to the next within the swarm cluster. Beeping is different from waggle dancing; it is a much faster way for the CLN and COIN members to convince their sisters of their idea by simply telling them that the time has come to move on to the new location. The bees being beeped at pick up the beep; consequently, they also slightly raise their body temperature, gradually increasing the temperature of the entire swarm. Once the swarm temperature is over a threshold—the tipping point—the swarm explodes, all bees start flying, and then, guided by the coolhunting bees, follow them to the new location of the hive.[7] There, the entire swarm gets down to business, and—turning into a Collaborative Interest Network (CIN)—starts building honeycombs and a new home for the hive.

The swarming of bees delivers a wonderful metaphor for cool-farming new trends. And there is even more that human coolfarmers can learn from the bees for each of the four steps: creator-COIN-CLN-CIN.

BEES AS CREATORS

Eating royal jelly. When a young queen bee has taken over a hive from her mother, she focuses in the first year on growing her swarm internally, laying eggs and producing many worker bees. In the second year, however, the worker bees usually pick and nurture a new queen. This new young queen grows out of an ordinary egg, but gets a special diet, the royal jelly, which turns her into a young queen instead of an ordinary worker bee. Something very similar happens in the human swarm. Aspiring CLN members are fed the human equivalent to royal jelly—critical knowledge—by older members of the swarm to make them full-fledged COIN core members.

We can find this process in many human coolfarmers. For example, when LEGO first introduced its Mindstorms set of programmable LEGO bricks, users were very quick in hacking and modifying the software. LEGO first wanted to defend its intellectual property and exclude hackers of Mindstorms software from developing their own improvements. But the company quickly discovered that encouraging and helping them to make their improvements would turn them into key members of the swarm, becoming both ambassadors and new product developers. LEGO therefore switched its strategy, supporting its Mindstorms hackers by publishing interfaces, and giving them access to its own developers and development tools—feeding them the royal jelly. Today, the company even gives the most active Mindstorms hackers free toolkits. In return, they have become scouts and trendsetters for the company, blazing new trails to build the coolest Mindstorms extensions—for free. The Mindstorms example is described in detail in Chapter 6.

Spreading the royal pheromone. In the bee world, bees distinguish between swarm members and outsider bees, which are not part of their own swarm, through the distinctive odor they get from their queen. This pheromone of the queen gives every bee of a swarm the typical smell of the swarm. When a stranger bee arrives at the hive, the guard bees check her smell, and if she does not carry the smell of the swarm, she is sent away. A foreign bee has a chance to bribe her way into the swarm, though, if she carries a full load of honey or pollen and offers it as a gift of entry. This is very similar to aspiring new COIN members offering their skills and knowledge as the gift of admission.

Once a queen does not give off enough pheromone anymore, the swarm chooses a new queen. The same is true for COINs. In the past, imperial leaders like Disney's Michael Eisner and Jack Welch at GE were spectacularly successful. But the time of regal leaders is over. To succeed in today's far more open and transparent economy, neither overpowering egos nor narrow skills as a lawyer or turnaround expert lead to success. Rather, the "pheromone" of a leader is his charisma suitable for the swarm. It is the combination of far-reaching vision combined with humility, modesty, personal warmth, and approachability. These are the attributes that build a successful team. For examples, look at master coolfarmers Linus Torvalds or Tim Berners-Lee, who both have shown plenty of pheromone. On the other hand, the Linux Debian distribution—the group of programmers developing one particular variant of Linux—has gone through a succession of leaders, shedding them when they ran out of pheromone. But like a successful hive, the Debian Linux community thrived by choosing a new queen that brought the right set of skills to move the Debian project forward at each phase along the way.

Doing the "waggle dance." The waggle dance is the most famous and best-researched part of the complex communication pattern of bees, winning Austrian researcher Karl von Frisch a Nobel Prize in Physiology or Medicine. The waggle dance is also an excellent way to allocate resources to tasks without a central leader. Because bees only have a limited number of workers to send out to collect pollen, scout bees are sent out first to find the most lucrative spots. These scout bees return to the hive and perform the waggle dance to tell their sisters where to find the nectar. New forager bees are recruited by dancing behind the scout until they learn the right movements. The waggle dance is really an elaborate marketing scheme. Waggle-dancing bees compete for the attention of their sisters, which stay at home in the hive. Each waggle dancer tries to attract the largest crowd of onlookers, to excite them to join them in their waggle dance. The larger and more accessible the potential honey source, the more excited and active the dance of the bee "selling" her honey source, and therefore, the more bees will follow her to the promised new source of pollen and nectar. Forager bees continue to follow the scout bee's dance until the nectar runs out or they find a more attractive dancer. This system allows the bees to seamlessly shift from one source to another without a leader or central command to slow the decision process.

The same is true for COINs. COIN members attract new members from the CLN and the CIN through waggle dancing, with the most active waggle dancers recruiting the most new members. When Tim Berners-Lee was presenting his World Wide Web system during a lunch break at the ACM Hypertext conference in San Antonio back in 1991, or when Linus Torvalds was sending out his initial e-mail to the Minix mailing list, they were doing one hell of a waggle dance. (We will be studying human waggle dancing in more detail in Chapter 3, on creators.)

But there is another application where bees use the waggle dance to communicate, with inspiring parallels to human coolfarmers.

When swarming, bees use the waggle dance to convey the location of the new hive to the swarm. Bee scouts (the coolhunters) inform their sisters of the attractions of the new hive in a two-step process: First, they do a waggle dance to win individual followers. Once the group of trendsetter bees is big enough, they build up the heat in the swarm. Human coolfarmers follow the same two-step process. In the first step, COIN members do a "waggle dance" to win new recruits for their cause in individual one-on-one interaction. When the core members of the COIN try to win new members in their friends and family network, they extend their COIN into a Collaborative Learning Network of new recruits. Some of the new recruits will, over time, join the original COIN, while others will be happy to remain users of the products of the COIN. Common to all of them is that they do the waggle dance, spreading the word and winning new recruits for their mission.

The OLPC (One Laptop Per Child) initiative is an example: "Queen bee" Nicholas Negroponte, the former director of the MIT Media Lab, started with a small team of a dozen volunteers. Their goal was to create a cost-effective alternative to the Microsoft Windows monopoly in Intel-based PCs and give children in the developing world a laptop tailored to their needs, at a much lower price. Negroponte and his original COIN did a lot of individual waggle dancing to win new recruits. While Negroponte toured the world, touting his idea at the World Economic Forum in Davos and talking to heads of state, his friend and trusted lieutenant Walter Bender was giving lots of one-on-one interviews in their small office at the MIT Media Lab to journalists and anyone else willing to listen— tons of waggle dancing.

The OLPC COIN has been growing rapidly. The core members still do a lot of "waggle dancing," but they also "beep" at the swarm to build up the heat. They are adding scores of open-source software developers and eager vendors of add-ons, growing a great Collaborative Learning Network. "Beeping at the swarm," they have also offered the OLPC to the American public at double the production price, in effect asking the public to co-sponsor another OLPC for a child in the developing world. Tens of thousands of Americans have taken up their offer, thus carrying the OLPC over the tipping point.

BEES AS COIN MEMBERS

COIN members are coolhunters. Once a bee swarm has decided to swarm and leave the hive with the queen and set up a new hive, it relies on the best coolhunters to look for the best location for a new home. They are not selected by the swarm, but decide on their own to go on their dangerous task. The same bees that go scouting for the new hive location were also the very best honey collectors. And the best of the best of these coolhunters, which return to report the new location they have found for the hive, are great coolfarmers, too. The most successful coolhunters, having found the best location, will do the most active waggle dance. They thus coolfarm the most new recruits to follow them to the new hive location and check it out for themselves.

The coolhunters are the elite of the swarm, the most experienced honey collectors. These scouts have been brought up in the hive under slightly higher temperatures than their less agile sisters. They get on their dangerous journey for a new hive not because the queen orders them to do so, but because they have been predisposed genetically and through their upbringing to be trendsetters. The same is true for human creators who nurture self-motivated trendsetters to join their swarm, their Collaborative Innovation Network. The goal is to grow a group of intrinsically motivated people who only care about the idea and the vision.

Successful venture capitalists are another example of coolfarmers who are also coolhunters. While venture capitalists traditionally hunt for cool business ideas, they are also instrumental in coolfarming the business ideas they invest in. But coolfarming is primarily about people, and secondly about ideas. When legendary venture capitalist John Doerr hunts for new business ideas, he hunts for people first and ideas second. While the cool idea certainly is the trigger, a cool idea is no good if the creators are not coolfarmers. Just compare Eduard-Leon Scott de Martinville with Thomas Alva Edison. John Doerr wants to find the Edisons and not the Martinvilles, the people who not only have cool ideas, but the people who can work with other people to farm their own cool ideas.

Bees switch roles. Bees assume different roles in their hive during their lifetime. In the first days of their adult life, the young bees take care of the hive by doing the menial task of cleaning the cells. Later, they tend to the brood, attend the queen, and receive nectar and pollen. Then, they build the honeycomb and ventilate the hive. Only as very mature and experienced individual bees do they get in touch with the outside world, initially as guards, making sure that only hive members are let in and keeping out intruders. In the very end, they become elite bees, the foragers, the pollen and nectar collectors necessary for the success of the hive.

The same is true for COIN members, who are expected to assume many different roles. Depending on the needs of the swarm, the COIN member is expected to be a honeycomb cleaner, a honeycomb builder, a swarm policeman, or a honey collector. Rarely is a new queen bee recruited as a queen bee. Usually, new COIN members join the group as peripheral members in the Collaborative Learning Network, attracted by the vision and the task at hand. They then work their way into the core of the COIN, learning from more seasoned members in this process. Only when they have shown their value to the hive will they become elite bees, coolhunters, and core COIN members.

For example, Alan Cox, the Welsh programmer who became Linus Torvalds's trusted lieutenant, and Ted Ts'o, the MIT student who still works on Linux full time, had many different roles during their more than ten years of Linux involvement. They started as novice programmers, became maintainers of critical modules, developed networking and other key functions for Linux, or even, in Alan's case, joined a commercial Linux vendor while still coordinating basic free-for-all, open-source development.

The swarm shapes the personality of the bee. Looking at the swarm from the outside, all the bees in it seem identical. Bee researchers tell us that this is absolutely not the case. First, while all the bees in a hive do have the same mother, they can have different fathers. When the queen bee leaves the hive for her mating flight, she mates with different drones. This means that bees inside a hive are either sisters or half-sisters. All other things being equal, bees prefer feeding bee larvae that are entirely genetically identical to them. This means that they prefer feeding larvae with which they share both mother and father, those that are their full sisters.

But for survival of the swarm, both homogeneity and diversity are needed. Besides having different genes from different fathers, bees have a second mechanism to ensure diversity and adaptability in the hive. Amazingly, bees can control the character of their young sisters. Depending on how warm it is inside the hive, young bees will turn into either long-lived laggards or short-lived workaholics. Bees have the capability to produce heat in the hive at will by eating honey and converting this excess energy into heat. They make use of this skill when they think that they will need eager honey collectors. If, on the other hand, the swarm needs to hibernate, the bees will turn down the heat, so their offspring will be much less active as honey collectors, but more long-lived.

Human swarms also define the character of their new additions. In the initial COIN phase, when the heat is on, worker bees buzz around. In the pressure-cooker environment of a start-up, young bees work very hard, but might burn out quickly. In the later phases, the heat in the COIN will be lower, particularly in the periphery, and bees will move at a more leisurely pace. In this more complacent environment with less excitement, new members stay around much longer. Just like in a beehive, there is no "one size fits all" approach; rather, the COIN needs to adapt the heat in the swarm to its current needs. The development of the personality of the bee is influenced by the needs of the COIN.

Motivation is in the DNA. A bee works all day, hence the saying "as busy as a bee." Why? In principle, a lazy bee could just stay put comfortably in the honeycomb all day, and indulge in the honey that her hardworking sisters have been hauling home. In fact, the male bees, the drones, are doing just that, eating honey and leading the good life, continuously on the lookout for a ready queen to have sex with. But they pay a heavy price. As soon as the hive decides they are no longer needed, they are kicked out mercilessly, and because they have never learned the tricks of hive maintenance and honey collection, they miserably starve to death. Their sisters, on the other hand, are extremely diligent and hardworking, moving up sequentially through the different job roles until they graduate to the highest level of being honey collectors. But why are they working so hard, instead of trying to lead the lazy life of their male brothers? The answer is really simple: They have been genetically hardwired to "just do it." Evolution has brought them to collaborate with each other for the benefit of the entire hive, with the hive becoming an extremely stable and long-living superorganism. Only if every bee does her duty will the entire hive flourish and grow, and the more and the better the bees are working together, the more the hive will thrive.

The same is true for COINs and CLNs of humans. For example, the Debian Linux distribution has lasted far longer than the creators who launched their free operating system more than ten years ago. When the Debian project was created, one of the first things its leaders did was to establish a code of conduct, called "the Debian constitution," laying out the ground rules of how the members of the Debian COIN and CLN deal with their own and with the outside world. They were, in effect, defining the genetic code of their swarm. The Debian community has gone through a whole succession of leaders, without changing its initial goals. And, in fact, it has flourished and held on to being one of the most dominant of the nonprofit Linux distributions. The initial genes planted by the first Debian creator have been highly successful in establishing a vibrant and long-lived hive. And as this hive has evolved, adding new genes through new queen bees, it has created a succession of Linux distributions while successfully competing with other hives in the form of other Linux distributions.

BEES AS CLN MEMBERS

Diverse hives are the most successful. While bees in a swarm are all sisters, there are still genetic differences between the bees, because the queen produces offspring from different fathers. Just like humans who prefer dealing with "people like us," a phenomenon known in science as "homophily," bees in the hive give preferential treatment to genetically identical sisters. For the hive as a superorganism, however, it is better to be genetically diverse, as research has shown that genetically diverse swarms do better. This means that there will be more half-sisters from many different fathers and fewer fully identical sisters in the beehive.

The same is true for Collaborative Innovation Networks. In a COIN, the recipe for creative ideas and innovation calls for accepting and even actively nurturing diversity. The same insights have been confirmed by our social network research, where we found that geographical proximity and diversity increase economic performance. When we analyzed the social network among researchers working at more than a hundred biotech start-ups in Massachusetts, we found that those start-ups that communicated with many competitors—and, even more important, with universities and outside research labs—did better than their less talkative peers.

Growing the community takes time and hard work. Occasionally, the beehive, the bee superorganism, splits, with half of the bees leaving the swarm and looking for a new homestead. So how do bees coolhunt and coolfarm their new hive when swarming? Once a swarm of bees has decided to leave the old hive, the bees cluster at a secure location, usually high up in a tree. This half of the swarm, which has left its old home, then sends out a few dozen scouts to go coolhunting for a suitable spot to set up a new home. The selection of these coolhunters is not done by the queen or the swarm. Rather, the most seasoned and experienced honey collectors take it upon themselves to venture out on this dangerous task, prospecting for a new hive, while the huge majority of the bees stay in the relative safety of the swarm, waiting at a temporary location.

Once scouts have found potential new homes, they report back to the swarm. When the coolhunters come back to the swarm, they need to convince their sisters of the positive properties of the new site for a new hive. The different coolhunter bees compete against each other, as each tries to convince the swarm of the relative merits of the new site she has discovered. Now, think of the new site for a new hive as a "trend." The most successful coolfarmer in the end convinces her sisters of the coolness of her trend, so the entire swarm will follow her lead and take off in that direction. Her task is to "coolfarm" the swarm, to get the swarm "over the tipping point." Toward that goal, she initially needs to win over new recruits one-on-one. Doing the waggle dance, she needs to convince a few sisters to go and check out the same location.

If the newly recruited coolhunters are similarly excited about the new location, they will come back and, in turn, start to waggle dance themselves, recruiting slowly increasing numbers of new coolhunters. This process of gradually growing the excitement takes time and hard work on the part of the bee scouts. Once a critical mass of coolhunters has been recruited, the swarm is ready to be brought over the tipping point and fly to the new location.

This is just like in the human world—where the core COIN members work to gradually build up buzz and excitement for their labor of love through recruiting new members. The process of recruiting new members involves one-on-one discussions with family members or with friends at the workplace (the Collaborative Learning Network); it entails writing blog posts, posting on online forums, or setting up a website. Initially the process will be slow, with outsiders investigating to learn more, a few people becoming interested enough to ask for more information, and even fewer deciding to become more actively involved. Over time, if the COIN stays around long enough and as the process gains momentum, the COIN will have recruited new members through its learning network to get to the next stage.

BEES AS CIN MEMBERS

Building the hive/getting the trend over the tipping point. For the bee swarm, this is the final phase where the bees fly from their temporary location to the chosen destination to set up the new hive. To trigger this final phase, "trendsetter" bees crawl through the swarm, turning up the heat until the swarm literally explodes and all bees take off to the new hive. The bee scouts, previously recruited by the original coolhunter of the new hive, become active agents of change at this point, only now, to get the entire swarm excited and over the tipping point, they use another technique.

Instead of doing individual, lengthy waggle dancing to convince the other bees, the trendsetter bees start making a beeping sound. They beep at other bees, telling them that the time has come to swarm. "Trust me," they seem to say, "I have found the perfect location for our new home. Just follow me, you will not regret it." The beeped-at bees start beeping also, slightly turning up their body heat. Step by step, the temperature of the entire swarm starts increasing, until it gets over a temperature threshold (the tipping point) and the trendsetter bees start herding the swarm in the right direction, pointing the way by rapidly flying back and forth between the more slowly flying swarm and the destination of the new hive. The swarm follows, finally ready to settle in at the new location and start building a new hive.

This process corresponds perfectly to the swarm building around a new trend, just before the trend takes off. That's the point where enthusiastic COIN members, reinforced by the members of the extended Collaborative Learning Network, become evangelists, building up the heat of the swarm until it explodes and infects the environment with its enthusiasm. Buzzing and beeping, they point the way, set the goals, and define the general direction. When interest grows wide enough, buzz building happens through newspaper interviews, articles, and even radio and TV shows.

How Apple launched its iPhone sets a fine example of how to fully leverage this process. Through systematic publicity leaks, "beeping at its swarm," Apple raised speculation and buzz about its product. The geek networks on Slashdot and other blogs provided a captive audience, following every move of Apple, speculating about features and availability of iPhones. When the iPhone finally came out, Apple could barely keep up with demand and had to restrict sales to two iPhones per customer.

Let's now refocus on how creative swarming differs from the well-known, well-planned, and well-studied project management process used by humans. Instead of going to the Western business world for more insights, we'll turn to Africa's emerging economies, where tribal structures and membership in the extended family—the swarm—still steer daily life of the individual and illustrate amazing facets of swarm creativity.

Swarm Creativity in Ghana

Ghana is not only the home country of former U.N. Secretary-General Kofi Annan, but also an emerging economy with some inspiring examples of collaborative innovation and learning. Kofi Annan displayed talents as a coolfarmer by managing, nurturing, and growing collaboration between the divergent interests of the 192 U.N. member states. But besides Annan, there are many other (though less illustrious) coolfarmers in Ghana, who nevertheless overcome seemingly insurmountable obstacles to build their COINs, CLNs, and CINs.

Today Ghana is one of the few success stories in black Africa. Corruption is much less rampant in Ghana than in the surrounding countries. While political life in Ghana is far from perfect, everything still works much better here than in the neighboring states of Ivory Coast, Burkina Faso, Togo, and Nigeria. This is partly due to the fact that Ghanaians have a strong sense of belonging to one community. Tribalism is still one of the main problems in Africa, with most citizens of a state associating not with their state, but with their tribe. While Ghana also consists of different tribes, the inhabitants of Ghana have a stronger national identity than people living in the surrounding countries.

Combining the communal culture of black Africa with strong efforts to become one of the leading economies of Africa by following a free-market approach, Ghana is a great test bed for discovering role models of swarm creativity. It offers an ideal laboratory setting where those role models stand out much more than they would in a well-established Western democracy with a well-functioning law system and a more mature and settled society. Ghana also stands out on the world happiness index as one of the countries in black Africa where the subjective well-being is comparatively high.[8] So the Ghanaians must be doing some things right.

Shipping computers from the Western world to schools in developing countries is what brought me to Ghana. I worked for ten years with an organization that collected used computers in Switzerland and brought them to Kenya. More recently, I extended the project to Ghana. It was in Ghana that I accidentally stumbled upon these role models of coolhunters and coolfarmers who were masterfully leveraging their Collaborative Learning and Interest networks to get their cool ideas off the ground. The role models include the Ghanaian founder of one of the first successful beach resorts in Ghana, the founder of one of the largest Internet cafes in Ghana, and a real coolfarmer who created a huge palm tree plantation in the middle of nowhere in rural Ghana. But before we focus on individual creators and coolfarmers, let's look at the environment of swarm creativity that is proliferating in Ghana.

ACCRA'S MAKOLA MARKET—SELF-ORGANIZATION AT ITS BEST

The way that the necessities of daily life are being traded in Ghana is a powerful example of swarm creativity. While the individuals in the small rural villages are self-reliant for most of their basic needs, they rely on the swarm when they need something special. In Ghana, the swarm assembles at the Makola market (see Figure 2–5).

Although there are Western-style supermarkets in Accra, Ghana's capital, where the tourist or expatriate from the Northern hemisphere can buy almost anything, that's not where Ghana's people shop for their food and any other imaginable goods. Rather, they go to the Makola market, an example of self-organization and swarm creativity.

FIGURE 2-5. Makola market teeming with life. Source: http://www.villasinghana.com/494.html.

The Makola market is not only at the heart of Accra, it literally is *the* heart of Accra. Located in the middle of the town, it is where 90 percent of Accra's inhabitants buy all their goods for daily life. Other than submarines and aircraft carriers, there is very little one cannot buy at Makola market. It is teeming with life; looked at it from the outside, it just seems noisy and chaotic. But like almost everything in Ghana, there is a pattern to it. There is no central control; each merchant booth is operated by its owner. At the top of the range are the established stores, where a room facing the street has been converted into a market stand. At the other end of the spectrum, little vendors display their wares on a blanket on the sidewalk. Heaps of shoes, staples of fresh and dried fish, live chickens, rows and rows of vegetables, fruit, and other types of food, schoolbooks, all sorts of cloths and fabrics, suitcases, and a myriad of other things form a chaotic composition of colors, smells, and textures that overwhelms the tourist.

For the expert visitor of the Makola market, though, it is actually quite easy to navigate the market. Each of the different types of goods and groceries occupies a distinct spot within the sprawling expanse. Vendors of vegetables, fruits, meat, or fish, but also of suitcases, clothes, shoes, or schoolbooks, have their preallocated locations. For example, there is an entire stretch of road where booth after booth sells nothing but schoolbooks. The advantages of this system are obvious. For customers, if they are looking for schoolbooks, they can head directly to the one row of stalls, one next to another, offering schoolbooks. Also, because the schoolbook vendors are all competing for the same customers, they keep prices low and equilibrium develops for the price of a particular book. But the system is also good for the vendors, because by pooling all their resources they are able to provide a much wider selection to the customers, who therefore will come from all over Ghana to the Makola market to buy their school supplies. This leads to a provisioning system rivaling in efficiency the shopping malls of the Western world, only at a fraction of the price. And even better, there is no central authority. What a great example of the power of the swarm!

I had the opportunity to experience the efficiency of this system for myself when our car suddenly broke down outside of Accra. Since we were about to head off on a sightseeing tour across Ghana, it was really unfortunate when the gearshift in the four-wheel-drive vehicle of my friend suddenly stopped working. The only gear still working was the reverse. Fortunately, this happened not too far from the home where I was staying, so we drove home backward!

My friend then called one of her Ghanaian friends for help. About two hours later he came by trotro—the private minibuses that make up the highly efficient public transportation system. He brought along a mobile car mechanic. Quickly, the mechanic located the broken part and took it out. Then he and the friend of my friend disappeared by trotro, traveling to a local street market, where they bought a generic, used spare part and temporarily fixed our car. Unfortunately, it did not fit too well, so oil was still leaking out. The next day, we drove to the used car parts market in Accra to try to find a suitable replacement part.

For more specialized goods there are various dedicated markets just outside the main Makola market, such as a huge market for selling used car parts (see Figure 2–6). There are hundreds of small entrepreneurs, each displaying his wares in a little stall. Booths

FIGURE 2–6. Used car parts market in Accra.

staffed by independent entrepreneurs display heaps of parts, either sorted by make or function. There are booths only selling used parts for Toyotas, Nissans, or Volkswagens, while other booths only sell mufflers or brake pads. The parts have been salvaged from old cars and car wrecks.

At first glance, it might seem that it would be better for an aspiring vendor of parts to be the only vendor of its kind, getting all the business. But looking more deeply, it makes absolute sense for the vendors to swarm together at one location, such that a mechanic trying to locate a particular part for a repair has a much bigger chance of actually finding the part he is looking for. There are even specialized "finders," mostly teenage boys who have memorized the inventory of the different used-parts suppliers, helping the prospective buyer of a car part locate the vendor who might have the particular part for sale—a sort of human search engine.

When we came to this market, one of the finder boys quickly guided us to the stalls selling parts for the Nissan truck of my friend. To further pin down our problem, we relied on the collective intelligence of the vendors, who noisily started discussing among themselves the different options of how to fix our car. In the end, the wisdom of the swarm converged on a particular part that they thought would best resolve our problem. As soon as we bought the part, another one of the mobile car mechanics showed up. For a small fee, he crept underneath our car and put in the new old clutch cable. Happily we drove away, once more convinced of the power of the swarm. Only, in this case, the story had a follow-up. It turned out that the part provided only a temporary fix for our problem; the clutch cable was still leaking oil, and we had to refill the clutch oil container every hundred kilometers.

In the end, we had no other choice but to go to the one and only authorized Nissan dealer in Accra. When the mechanic in the repair shop looked up our car make and model in an online database to locate the car part, he found that our car had been manufactured for Europe, while the parts that were available in Ghana came from Nissans manufactured in Japan. Obviously there were some slight differences between the two model types, which both the finder boys and the group of vendors at the used car parts market had failed to notice and probably could not know. So in this case, while the swarm temporarily fixed the problem, it was twenty-first-century Internet technology that in the end solved the puzzle.

Solving this problem required both the members of the swarm collaborating to solve the problem and the means to access the global knowledge base.

Put another way, the lesson is simply this: Working together and pooling resources benefits everybody: suppliers, dealers, and customers.

PUBLIC TRANSPORTATION BY SWARM CREATIVITY

The public transportation system in Ghana is another wonderful example of swarm creativity. Until very recently there was no "official" bus system in Ghana, but the unofficial system of minibuses, called "trotro," works quite well. The trotro network covers the entire country, permitting travelers to get to any location within Ghana cheaply and quickly. I tried it out myself, using a trotro for the same route I had previously driven with my friend's Nissan truck. The trotro from Anloga, a fishermen's town on the coast right at the border with Togo, took less than four hours to get me back to Accra at a cost of less than two dollars—a fare that probably already included a hefty price hike just for tourists. When driving ourselves, it had taken us at least six hours to get from Anloga to Accra and the house of my friend.

What I found most amazing is that the demand-and-supply adjustment system worked so well, because whenever people were looking for a trotro, it seemed that at least one, and sometimes many, of the minibuses were available, anywhere in Ghana.

On a hot and steamy morning I went with my Ghanaian friend to the "37" trotro hub in Accra (shown in Figure 2–7) to learn more about how the system operates. The trotro hub is a huge walled-in place of dusty mud, overcrowded with people, little buses, and taxis. Like ants coming and going to their hive on ant roads, hundreds of trotros enter the huge place in a never-ending stream, while at the exit a similar stream of vans pours out. Inside the place, the little buses seem to cover every inch. What available space is

FIGURE 2–7. The trotro "37" hub in Accra.

not taken up by trotros is plastered with little booths where street vendors sell drinks, dried fruits, pastries, sunglasses, newspapers, mobile phone cards, and all the others things travelers might need. Besides the minibuses and the sales booths, passengers squeeze by, always ready to jump to the side when a trotro inches by to its destination, wherever that might be. From a bird's-eye view, the entire station would look like the proverbial anthill, with little buses, sales booths, and passengers all chaotically intermingled, without a recognizable pattern. But there is a highly efficient system underlying the trotro operation.

On this steamy Thursday morning I talked with trotro drivers and passengers, trying to understand how the system works. And I became more and more impressed with what I learned. Sometimes my Ghanaian friend had to translate to English, because the drivers only spoke their native Akan language. In the end we were directed to a "bookman" sitting in a little cabin in a corner of the huge place. He was a slim and aged man with wise old eyes. Talking in Akan, he explained the system. As a "bookman," he is a coordinator of sorts, allocating passengers to the minibuses. All trotros are unionized, which means that each trotro driver has to choose and join a union. This particular morning the bookman we were talking to was managing the highly lucrative routes to the Tema region, the second largest city in Ghana after Accra and its industrial capital.

Every morning, a trotro driver checks in with his union "bookman," paying his daily fee and registering with his license plate number. He is then entered onto a list and allocated to one of the sub-destinations within the Tema region. As there are profitable and less desirable destinations, unions alternate between different spots at the different stations. As our bookman explained to us, under this alternating schedule, his union would only get the Tema spot at station "37" again eight days from now. Tomorrow, he would manage another spot with other destinations at another trotro station.

At the Tema spot at the "37" station, a wooden sign listing the destination is put on top of the bus and behind the dashboard. At the same time, the drivers or their helpers are endlessly shouting out the destination, because a large number of passengers are not able to read the signs. Once a bus is filled with passengers, the signs are removed and placed inside or on top of the next bus allocated to the same destination by the bookman, while the filled bus inches out of the "37" station, through a cacophony of yelling and honking bus drivers and street vendors, squeezing by other buses, taxis, sales booths, and passengers.

Once on the road, trotro drivers are feared for their reckless way of driving. As time is money, they do everything they can to get to their destination as quickly as possible, so they can pick up another load of passengers. However, if they have dropped off some of their passengers on the way, the naked arm of the helper waves out of the passenger side window, indicating to people waiting on the street that the trotro has vacant seats. If they wave back, the trotro pulls over and picks them up. This leads to a system that looks highly chaotic from the outside because the trotro drivers alternate between driving like madmen and idling along. In actuality, each driver is trying to reach his destination as quickly as possible, while at the same time searching for new passengers on the road.

Overall, the trotro is an extremely efficient transportation system covering all of Ghana, and it is entirely based on swarm creativity and self-organization. For a fraction of a dollar, destinations within Accra can be easily reached, while tickets to remote towns cost a few dollars. Through their unions, trotro drivers make sure that every driver gets fair access to passengers and the most lucrative routes. The state interferes very little; its main role is to check and certify road safety of vehicles and the driving capabilities of drivers. This means that with no external control, trotro drivers self-organize and collaborate in a highly cost-effective system with every driver being his own entrepreneur, in charge of his own destiny.

When I had already returned to Switzerland, I heard that one of my Ghanaian friends had just had a very bad car accident with a trotro. While driving in her passenger car to the farm where she was the manager, she had collided with a reckless trotro driver. While she was only slightly injured, the trotro had been irreparably damaged, and the entire busload of passengers had been seriously hurt.

There is, then, a drawback to this kind of self-organization, if each trotro driver wants to maximize income for himself by driving as rapidly as possible. If there is a balance between serving the public good and optimizing his own gain, this driver tried to tip the scale too much toward himself, with very bad consequences for himself and his passengers. As we will see over and over again, *if you are too selfish, swarm creativity will break down.*

FIVE QUICK GHANAIAN LESSONS ON SWARM CREATIVITY

I frequently noticed in Ghana that while someone was trying to do the best for me, his failure to explain his reasoning converted the result into the opposite. Sometimes the motivations on both sides are not really clear. Our experience at the beach restaurant in the romantic Axim beach resort is an example.

Lesson 1: Keep information flowing within the swarm. It is no easy thing to get ice cream in Ghana. Electricity breaks down all the time, and frequently it is turned off for half a day, which makes it difficult to keep ice cream in its frozen state for extended periods of time. So we were pleasantly surprised when the menu of our beach hotel in Axim offered ice cream. When we ordered our ice cream from the waiter, we chose chocolate and strawberry. We were slightly surprised when the restaurant manager himself proudly brought us mixed strawberry and vanilla ice cream. We informed him that we had ordered strawberry and chocolate; he deeply apologized and promised to bring us what we had ordered.

We saw him throw away the strawberry and vanilla ice cream and head back to the restaurant kitchen. But a few seconds later he was back, even more apologetic, telling us that the chocolate had melted in the hot Ghanaian climate and that strawberry and vanilla was all that was still available. The chef had decided, on his own, that substituting vanilla for chocolate was what we'd want. Of course, the chef had guessed right—we were starving to get some cold ice cream—but the chef had not bothered to inform the hotel manager about our original order and the changes he had made without asking us. In the end, we gladly accepted a new vanilla and strawberry, but the wasted ice cream was a heavy price to pay in a country where ice cream is such a highly valued rare treat.

Lesson 2: Try to anticipate the incentives of the swarm. In the same restaurant, we experienced a second communication breakdown and cultural misunderstanding. One day I told the waiter I wanted a chef's salad as a starter for the three of us—my two kids and I would share one salad (since we were not that hungry) and then would also have a second dish each for lunch. And indeed I got a large, heaping plate of salad as the first course of our lunch. The not-so-pleasant surprise came afterward, when the waiter doubled the price of the salad—explaining that I had asked for a "big" salad. He claimed he had only tried to follow my wishes and could not understand why I refused to pay the double price.

Lesson 3: You cannot force people into membership in the swarm. I also took my children to the small town of Axim. Axim is an old city with a historic slave castle, which my children and I visited before embarking on a walk around the small town, looking at the street vendors and their stalls lining the sides of the street. While I was quite fascinated by the bustling street life, I was surprised to learn that my kids were less than taken with the colorful scenery. They found the streets and houses very dirty and the smell coming from the open sewage canals disgusting. The kids were right in one respect: Red dust was indeed everywhere because the streets are mostly unpaved, and the canals, well, stank. But I found the scenery so full of life that I could have watched it for a long time. Not so my kids. After a ten-minute walk, and after quickly drinking a cold Coke from one of the street vendors, they insisted on taking a taxi back to the hotel as quickly as possible.

Lesson 4: It's amazing how the swarm can fix things. At the end of our beach holiday we drove back from Axim to Accra. Our friends had sent their Nissan truck with a driver to pick us up at the beach resort. On the drive back, as we were near the old capital of Ghana, Cape Coast, our driver suddenly pulled the car in a filling station, telling us that he had noticed a strange sound. I walked around the car and saw that one of the tires was flat. At the filling station, however, they told us that they were only equipped to pump gas and could not exchange our spare tire. Without comment, our driver disappeared, taking the car keys with him. We could do nothing but wait in the hot sun and make sure that our belongings left in the unlocked car stayed where they were.

We were very relieved when fifteen minutes later our driver came back, bringing with him a powerfully built young man in mechanic's overalls. The young man then searched for our car jack, which, it turned out, was not working. The young man now disappeared, and twenty minutes later, he came back with an old car jack. Ten minutes later our spare tire was put properly in place and we could resume our trip. I then asked our driver if it would be possible to have our flat tire fixed immediately. He assured me that it would be no problem, and a few minutes later he pulled over at what appeared to me to be a tiny shack in the midst of a large collection of small market stands along the road. Our particular stand had four broken tires heaped in front of it. It turned out the wiry little man in the shack was operating a bustling flat-tire fixing business. Using only the most primitive tools, he plugged the hole in our tire in no time and put the tire back on the rim. Then, with the single sophisticated piece of equipment he had, a fuel-operated compressor, he inflated our tire.

Lesson 5: Sharing with the swarm can lead to bruises. While the driver and I were standing outside the car and waiting to have our flat tire repaired, my children inside the car were eating candy. When they saw a few kids approaching, they threw some of the shrink-wrapped candy to them. At first, the kids did not know what to do with the little square pieces wrapped in glittering aluminum foil, but as soon as one of them had unwrapped the candy and put it into her little mouth, a delighted smile lit up her face. More children started flocking to the car, and then even some teenagers joined them.

My children were busy throwing candy out of the car window, but then things started getting out of control. The swarm of kids became more aggressive, banging at the car door, so I started getting worried for my friend's car. I took the bag of candies and stepped away from the car. Now the entire swarm of about twenty children, aged from three to sixteen years, was surrounding me. I could not get out the candies fast enough for them. Hands were reaching out and touching me everywhere. By now even some adults were joining in. In the end a tall guy, probably half a head taller than I am (and I am over six feet), wrestled the torn bag out of my hand. The rest of the candy fell on the ground and the swarm started fighting over it. Thirty seconds later all the candies were gone, and another few seconds later the swarm had dissolved. The only thing remaining was some discarded candy paper lying on the ground.

Sometimes the swarm can get out of control—in particular if the protocol of sharing with the swarm has not been previously established.

Overall, daily life in Ghana is teaching some important lessons in swarm creativity and about what works and what does not. After this introduction into grassroots swarm creativity, both from the perspective of human swarms in Africa and looking at the way swarms of honeybees do their coolfarming, we are now ready to put together the essentials of coolfarming.

Essentials of Coolfarming and Coolhunting

If you want to be a successful coolfarmer, here are the main aspects to consider. The trick is to "be a bee," both as a creator (i.e., a leader) and as a COIN member (i.e., a team player). Table 2–1 summarizes the coolfarming process described in this chapter. As a creator of a new idea, you have to eat lots of royal jelly; that is, you have to stand on the shoulders of giants and learn from others. You also

Table 2-1. Coolfarming and coolhunting at a glance.

	Creator	COIN (Collaborative Innovation Network)	CLN (Collaborative Learning Network)	CIN (Collaborative Interest Network)
Be a Bee	Eat royal jelly Mark your swarm with royal pheromone Waggle dance	Be a coolhunter Switch roles Add the right genes	Build community Require diversity	Build the hive
Goal	Be a swarm leader	Be a team player	Find the influentials	Find the buyers
Task	Innovate Build the vision	Collaborate Build the product	Communicate Build the buzz	Build the market
Cool-hunting	Leader	Builders	Influentials	Buyers

have to diffuse lots of royal pheromone to mark your swarm and distinguish your idea from the idea of others. Both as a creator and COIN member it is essential to waggle dance, to recruit suitable—but intrinsically motivated—new candidates. In the first phase, the creator is the innovator, the "flag bearer" of the vision, which is collaboratively realized and put into place by the COIN. Once the COIN has developed, COIN members have to become coolhunters, hunting both for new COIN members and cool new ideas to further develop the core product.

Once a first prototype of the product has been developed by the COIN, the team has to show it off to friends and family in a Collaborative Learning Network. This CLN, which should be as diverse as possible, acts both as a feedback system to refine the product and as a springboard for viral marketing. The goal is to grow the community by finding external influentials until the community is strong enough to take on a business life of its own, finding the buyers for its product. Master coolfarmers make the product "cool" to the community by making sure there is something "in it" for each member of the community. The CLN then adopts the output of the COIN, making it its own, and communicates the excitement to the outside world, this way building the buzz. In the end, a Collaborative Interest Network finally springs to life, evangelized and fueled by the members of the CLN. The CIN growing around Linux illustrates that there is indeed something very cool in it for every Linux user, namely, a free operating system.

The bottom-most row in Table 2–1 indicates that the coolfarming process can also be used for coolhunting, or spotting the next cool trend. The trick is to look first for the creator (the leader of the swarm), next for the COIN (the team that will build the trend), then for the CLN (the group of influencers who will raise the buzz), and then, finally, for the CIN (the buyers of the cool new product). The sooner along the coolfarming process you can identify this emergent pattern, the better you can time and plan your own actions.

One open question is whether coolfarming can be beneficially employed in the pursuit of small businesses, or if these methods are only good for organizations of larger size with more than twenty members. The answer is that coolfarming works for organizations of any size. If the team is smaller than, say, five to eight people, those people need to search and coolhunt—as larger organizations also should—outside their team for further trends and trendsetters to reinforce the original team.

All of the business examples in this chapter started as a swarm business, catering to the needs of an emergent swarm without a clear understanding of what the future business model would be. The founders of these businesses had a vision, and they did not hesitate to make it come true—although initially they had no clue how they ever would be able to recoup their investments. In the end, however, catering to the needs of their swarm, they turned them into a resounding success.

The next four chapters describe the four-step coolfarming process—creator-COIN-CLN-CIN—in detail.

3

Creators
Building the Vision

Per aspera ad astra: "Over the stones [obstacles] to the stars."

LEADERS OF INNOVATION networks are not leaders in the conventional sense. They are not imperial. They are not the best in everything they do. They do not know it all, nor do they claim to know it all. People like Tim Berners-Lee (creator of the Web), Linus Torvalds (creator of the Linux operating system), and Roy Fielding (founder of the Apache Software Foundation, developers of the highly popular web server) are of an entirely different ilk. The members of their swarms follow their leader's call because they share the same calling.

When Linus Torvalds started Linux sometime in 1991, he sent out the following e-mail:[1]

From: torvalds@klaava.helsinki.fi (Linus Benedict Torvalds)
To: Newsgroups: comp.os.minix
Subject: What would you like to see most in minix?
Summary: small poll for my new operating system

Hello everybody out there using minix-

I'm doing a (free) operating system (just a hobby, won't be big and professional like gnu) for 386 (486) AT clones. This has been brewing since april, and is starting to get ready. I'd like any feedback on things people like/dislike in minix, as my OS resembles it somewhat (same physical layout of the file-system due to practical reasons) among other things.

I've currently ported bash (1.08) an gcc (1.40), and things seem to work. This implies that I'll get something practical within a few months, and I'd like to know what features most people want.

Any suggestions are welcome, but I won't promise I'll implement them :-)

Linus Torvalds torvalds@kruuna.helsinki.fi

As you can see, Torvalds informally appealed to like-minded people to join him in his venture. But his leadership was not ironclad. Linus himself says, "I can't afford to make too many stupid mistakes, because then people watching will say, hey, maybe we can find someone better. I don't have any authority over Linux other than this notion that I know what I'm doing."[2]

Because of the unique nature of innovation networks, COIN leaders can afford to be indecisive. Members of his swarm say this about Torvalds: "Often, when things are on the verge of getting messy, he'll consciously avoid making a decision, allowing time for feelings to dissipate. Eventually, some obvious solution will come to the fore or the issue will just fade away."[3] Knowing when *not* to do anything and just letting things slip is a very important skill for a COIN leader. In a networked world, leaders of COINs try hard to make themselves unnecessary. They don't pretend to be the best in all disciplines.

The power of a COIN leader is based on nothing more than the collective respect of his cohorts. Torvalds says, "To be honest, the fact that people trust you gives you a lot of power over people. Having another person's trust is more powerful than all other management techniques put together. I have no legal or explicit power. I only have the power of having people's trust—but that's a lot of power."[4] What matters is personal integrity, trustworthiness, and willingness to communicate transparently and honestly.

COIN Leaders Are *Not* Leaders

We sometimes find leaders of this type in Fortune 100 companies, with great results for the companies they are leading. Why do Boeing and Procter & Gamble outperform their peers?[5] It's not because they invented superior new products, or because they have a more talented sales force, or because they better optimized their supply chain. It's because they work as a swarm, where each bee shares "DNA"; that is, they share not only goals and a vision, but also a style of working together. Collaboration in the swarm starts at the top, with the queen bee. CEOs like A. G. Lafley of Procter & Gamble or W. James McNerney Jr. of Boeing are archetypes of a new model of leaders, sharing many traits with COIN leaders like Linus Torvalds. They see themselves foremost as team builders and coolfarmers. This style is very different from the imperial command-and-control CEOs of the past. Rather, it is a "trust-and-let-go" style of leadership, where, once the goals have been set, the team members are mostly on their own

FIGURE 3–1.
Leaders of a
COIN are like
pilots of a
balloon.

in reaching the goal. Bertrand Piccard, the first person to orbit earth by balloon, likens this new type of leader to the pilot of a balloon (Figure 3–1). This is a great analogy, so let's take a closer look.

When flying a balloon, the only factor the pilot can influence is the timing of the start and the height of the balloon. Before starting on her balloon journey, she can check the weather forecast and look for favorable weather conditions and winds that hopefully carry her where she wants to go. This way she avoids foreseeable storms, or the risk of being hit by lightning. Of course, there is no 100 percent guarantee that the forecast will be accurate and the weather as favorable as predicted. If she suddenly gets into rough weather and wind currents start carrying her to the wrong place, the only option she has is to change the elevation of the balloon. By shedding ballast or releasing gas in the balloon, she can either raise or lower her flying height. This is really the only thing she can do, once she has embarked on her journey.

Leaders of the past saw themselves as drivers at the steering wheel of a race car, controlling every aspect of the group or enterprise they were supposed to lead, setting the speed precisely, and steering the corporate car precisely to where they thought it should go. COIN creators are very different. Like balloon pilots, they set the cornerstones and the big vision and then let the COIN members take over. They can try to set a course by following favorable wind currents, but once they have decided on a height, they are dependent on the wind. The only thing they still have the power to do is adjust the height to catch a more favorable wind. To get higher, they have to shed ballast. But like balloon pilots, they cannot do that too many times, because they have only a very limited amount of ballast they can get rid of. Once they have thrown off the ballast, the only other thing they can still do to gain altitude is add gas to the balloon by increasing the pressure. But again, they cannot increase the pressure too much, otherwise the balloon will explode. If, on the other hand, they need to get lower, to evade a thunderstorm or catch better winds, they can release gas in the balloon. They have to be careful, though, as their supply of gas is very limited. If they release too much gas, they will not have enough to gain height again.

> **COOLFARMING LESSON: Creators must be able to let go.** Balloon pilots know that it is awfully hard not to be able to directly control the direction of where the balloon is heading. But this is precisely what leaders of COINs do. They decide on a course, they map out the direction, they get together a team that will fly the balloon, but once the flight has taken off, then they cannot do much but enjoy the ride.

Eating and Feeding Royal Jelly

Besides being like balloon pilots, creators are also like bees, as discussed in earlier chapters. To grow their hive, young bees first have to eat royal jelly; later on they will feed it to their brood. The longer a young bee is eating royal jelly, the stronger it gets. If she gets it for more than two days, she will become a queen. Creators, the queen bees in their innovation beehive, are eating royal jelly, too.

Creators are great consumers and distributors of knowledge—the ultimate royal jelly. Isaac Newton was not just feeding royal jelly to others, but also feasting on it when he famously said, "If I have seen further it is by standing on the shoulders of giants." During Microsoft's feud with Linux and the open-source movement, when Craig Mundie, Microsoft's VP of research, accused Linux of plagiarizing and free riding on the work of others, Linus Torvalds wrote in an e-mail response: "I wonder if Mundie has ever heard of Sir Isaac Newton? He's not only famous for having set the foundations for classical mechanics (and the original theory of gravitation, which is what most people remember, along with the apple tree story), but he is also famous for how he acknowledged the achievement: If I have been able to see further, it was only because I stood on the shoulders of giants. . . . I'd rather listen to Newton than to Mundie. He may have been dead for almost three hundred years, but despite that he stinks up the room less."[6]

Creators are constantly learning and adapting from others. Once again, Linus Torvalds puts it very succinctly, "To invent something totally new and different just because you want to do something new and different is, in my opinion, the height of stupidity and hubris. Linux is doing great things exactly because Linux isn't throwing out the baby with the bathwater, like so many projects tend to want to do. The NIH syndrome [Not Invented Here] is a disease."[7]

On the other hand, Torvalds does not go out and consciously dissect and analyze competing operating systems. For example, computer vendor Sun Microsystems, which had a competing Unix operating system (OS) called Solaris, decided to open-source Solaris to level the playing ground. Torvalds was asked in an interview if he worried about Solaris taking over Linux's role, and whether he would try to integrate as many great features from Solaris into Linux as possible. His answer was that he had better things to do than look at other operating systems. Rather, he would be waiting for people who know Solaris better than he does to tell him what great features they wanted to have integrated into the next version of the Linux OS.

> **COOLFARMING LESSON: Creators constantly learn from their environment.**
> This is precisely the advantage of living in an ecosystem of COINs and CLNs, learning networks that filter information and knowledge, allowing the leader of the COIN to focus on the essentials. Like young bees, creators and COIN members are being fed the royal jelly (i.e., critical knowledge) by members of their swarm, digesting what they are being taught, shaping and molding it in the process. By adding their own interpretation and ideas to the royal jelly they get from their spiritual ancestors, they create the new ideas and innovations that later on will spawn a new swarm. Examples of collaborative innovators applying this process abound. Tim Berners-Lee took the ideas from his spiritual forebears like Vannevar Bush—who described the hyperlinking concept first—and Ted Nelson—who coined the term *hypertext*. Or look at Steve Jobs, who, as a young kid doing odd technical jobs at high-tech start-ups in the Silicon Valley, saw early versions of personal computers, the computer mouse, and windowing systems at the famous Xerox PARC research lab in Palo Alto. Based on this infusion of royal jelly, Jobs and Steve Wozniak went on to start Apple Computer.

Royal Pheromone—Nicholas Negroponte

Nicholas Negroponte, the legendary founder and longtime chairman of the MIT Media Lab, is a master of waggle dancing, and both eating and feeding royal jelly. But there is a second ingredient that keeps the swarm together—the royal pheromone of the bee queen. As we have seen before, the pheromone of the queen is what gives the swarm its distinctive odor, thereby permitting the guards at the entrance to the hive to weed out members not belonging to the swarm. Just like the bee queen, creators of cool new trends also need to be able to diffuse "royal pheromone."

"Royal pheromone" is the distinctive something, hard to pin down but absolutely essential, that gives identity to the swarm. This identity can come through a charismatic leader, through the collective intelligence of the core COIN team, or through some external symbols important to swarm members. Most of the time, the royal pheromone will be a mix of the three. Most important, though, will be the behavior of the leader. In that respect, Nicholas Negroponte is a great role model. He is first and foremost a computer and media visionary, and his talent for salesmanship enabled him to succeed in creating the MIT Media Lab from nothing and then making it, over the course of its first ten years, the most revolutionary and well-known research lab at MIT. The only thing Negroponte had, when starting the Media Lab, was his vision, and he used a diagram of three interconnected rings, known as the "teething rings," to show the lab's overlapping interests in computers, broadcasting, and publishing.[8]

Obviously, a successful creator needs strong self-esteem, well grounded in reality. However, in an interview, Nicholas Negroponte was asked whether he was prone to megalomania. His answer was: "Not really. But I want to do things on a large scale in order to have impact. That's one of the reasons why the Media Lab is the way it is. My megalomania is not egocentric. It's more about trying to do things big, because if it's not big, it's not worth your time."[9]

This is true for each creator of a COIN. Whether it is Thomas Alva Edison, Tim Berners-Lee, Linus Torvalds, or Nicholas Negroponte, they all set out to change the world. Steve Jobs said it very succinctly, when in 1983, he offered the job of Apple CEO to then Pepsi CEO John Sculley: "Do you want to spend the rest of your life selling sugared water, or do you want a chance to change the world?" With this ambition, the main way for creators to attract new members to their COIN is their "royal pheromone." Only by sharing his vision, and doing a continuous waggle dance, could Nicholas Negroponte convince new sponsors to come up with the millions of dollars needed to start the Media Lab. At the same time, he also needed to convince leading computer science professors, such as artificial intelligence (AI) pioneers Marvin Minsky and Seymour Papert, to join the Media Lab as faculty. Obviously, he did a phenomenal job waggle dancing and diffusing royal pheromone. As a leader of his COIN—the Media Lab—Negroponte's reachability was legendary. One of the few times he got angry was when a new employee at the Media Lab told callers he was on vacation in his summer home in Greece. Negroponte does not go on vacation; he just is physically at another location, but always reachable over the net.

More recently, he has put his talents to new use, almost single-handedly creating the OLPC—One Laptop Per Child—with the goal of putting an affordable laptop, initially scheduled to cost less than $100, into the hand of every child in the world. As the creator of the OLPC idea, he once more used his proven ability to diffuse royal pheromone. When, in 2005, he first announced the idea to develop a laptop rugged enough to survive continued use by children in developing countries, and cheap enough to be bought or sponsored for rural schools in those countries, he was decried as an illusionary dreamer asking for the impossible. Barely three years later, more than 600,000 of the laptops already had been sold (as of August 2008), although it probably costs anywhere between $130 and $150 to manufacture them. Along the way, a revolutionary new display technology was developed, as well as a new operating system and a set of student-friendly applications, based on the Linux OS. At the same time, the OLPC has spawned a whole new industry of ultralight and cheap laptops priced below $200.

Negroponte first announced the OLPC at, of all places, the 2005 World Economic Forum in Davos. He kept up the buzz and excitement with a continuous stream of updates on the OLPC, addressing the media jointly with luminaries such as U.N. Secretary-General Kofi Annan at events such as the United Nations summit on technology in Tunisia. When he travels, he always leaves a pheromone trail behind—always being fully connected to the net, always taking two laptops along. Negroponte not only loves his job, he lives and breathes it eighteen hours a day, seven days a week. There is no boundary between his work and his life. In his own words, he is a proponent of the "omelet theory of life."[10] Some people live a fried egg life, where they separate the yolk and the white, with work being the yolk and life being the clearly distinct white. Negroponte's life is an omelet.

> **COOLFARMING LESSON: Creators never cease to be on a mission.**
> Negroponte's pheromone trail is laid by living life with a mission. Currently, his mission is the OLPC. He is unbelievably passionate about it and demonstrates his full commitment by showing off his labor of love to anybody willing to listen, anytime, and anywhere, and declaring that it is "unquestionably for me my most important project—and it's the one I'll do for the rest of my life."[11]

Coolfarmers Are Coolhunters

To grow their cool idea, coolfarmers also have to be coolhunters, continuously looking for new ideas to extend their original vision, and for new cool people whom they would like to recruit to join them on their endeavor. While continuously selling his OLPC passion, Nicholas Negroponte is also a great coolhunter of talent and ideas, recruiting people like Walter Bender, a senior researcher at the MIT Media Lab, to lead the development of Sugar, the revolutionary operating system used with the OLPC, or Mary Lou Jepsen, the one-time OLPC chief technology officer, who invented a radically new type of display for the OLPC. Both of these innovations, Sugar, a Linux-based open source operating system with a kid-friendly user interface (the inventors call it a desktop environment), and the new display that can be produced more cheaply, works with less energy, and is readable even in bright sunlight, were invented by passionate COIN members on a shoestring budget.

Mark Hunter—also known as "The Cobra Snake"—is a totally different type of coolhunter. In no time this young man built a reputation as a hipster and one of the main trendsetters on the party scene. When he was less than twenty years old, Mark started sneaking into trendy parties in Los Angeles, armed with a digital camera, snapping pictures of the likes of Paris and Nicky Hilton, and then posting the pictures on his website every night. For anybody wanting to be hip to the party scene of LA and NYC, there is no substitute for being on Hunter's photo blog. His talent for spotting cool people and taking their picture is amazing, making his website, thecobrasnake.com, a cornerstone of party picture sites. In the meantime, Hunter has cashed in on the popularity of his site, selling a line of T-shirts, and he doesn't have to sneak into parties anymore. Instead, he is paid to be the official picture taker at parties in LA and fashion meccas such as New York, London, Tokyo, and Paris.

But why is he that successful? As the *Los Angeles Times* put it in an article about him, "All Hunter does is go out at night, take pictures of people who catch his eye, and then post the photos on his website."[12] By his own admission, Hunter is not physically striking and is somewhat goofy. And still he is probably the most preeminent hipster in LA.

The simple explanation for his success is that he is an excellent coolfarmer. He is giving away things for free. To be more precise, he takes zillions of pictures of young people at parties and posts them, for free, on his website. He makes it easy to link to his pictures, print them out, and use them for other purposes. Girls take his pictures to the hairdresser to get their hair cut in a particular style. Fashion labels use his pictures for advertisement of their apparel. Kids are using them as an inspiration to design their own outfits. Giving away his original product has worked beautifully for The Cobra Snake.

Hunter owes his popularity both to his talent as a photographer of people and his persistence. As a photographer, he has developed a style of taking pictures from the other angle, the one we would never have seen, showing people (and often celebrities) in a totally new light. Just like Nicholas Negroponte, Hunter is not doing a job; he is on a mission. His mission is to frenetically shoot pictures. As soon as he arrives at a party, he starts snapping pictures constantly so that he won't miss that one unique shot. This way he became one of the most eminent photo bloggers in the world.

Hunter also wants to make us—both his audience and his target—look cool. According to the *LA Times*, Hunter once wrote: "People try to look cool for a reason, to get noticed, but they put so much effort into their look and they should get more out of it." This means he is trying to get his photo targets to look cool, hip, outrageous, or beautiful. In some sense, Hunter is an arbiter of fashion, taking the pictures of people who are extremely attractive, extremely unattractive, or extremely well dressed. When asked why he is doing this, he says, "I want to have good vibes with people. With enough free love that I'm giving out, I would hope it would come back eventually." Like all successful coolhunters and coolfarmers, Hunter also has a very positive attitude to life. In his own words, "That's what's so exciting about the time we're in right now. There's so much space for creativity."[13]

Hunter also has shown other talents as a coolfarmer, by discovering Cory Kennedy and making her his intern in 2005. Since then, Cory has become far more successful as a hipster partygoer than even Mark Hunter himself. As of August 21, 2008, Cory's Wikipedia entry was forty-four lines compared to Mark's five lines.

When Mark first spotted Cory at a rock concert, he did nothing but take her picture, as he had done with hundreds of girls before. He uploaded her pictures to his website, immediately recognized her picture appeal, and offered her an unpaid internship. Snapping many more pictures of her in the succeeding months turned her into an immediate Internet celebrity. People-watchers from Norway to Japan followed her exploits, imitated her unique clothing style, and visited her website. Cory became famous because people who watched Mark Hunter also started watching her. It soon became clear that Cory's childlike face, surrounded by LA hipster accessories, had its own gravitational pull.

Once Mark recognized that Cory's pictures helped draw more visitors to his site, he started to take even more pictures of her and featuring his favorite subject prominently on his site. As one blogger wrote, "I can't take my eyes off of her. She's got something that intrigues me."[14] Hunter noticed that whenever he put up a new picture of Cory he got a spike in page hits coming from fashion community sites. As Mark already had connections into the fashion model scene, he started marketing Cory as a model, knowing that acting as her gatekeeper and photographer would also increase his standing in this community. After the first model shooting for Nylon, a fashion magazine, people started recognizing her on the street. Her celebrity status skyrocketed, with real-world model work and Internet presence reinforcing each other. Barely sixteen, Cory was now being paid $100 per night just to show up at clubs and parties. Paris Hilton and Lindsay Lohan were inviting her as a special guest to their parties. Today, her career as a fashion model and aspiring actress seems unstoppable. Her MySpace page has over one million friends.

> **Coolfarming Lesson: To succeed as a coolfarmer one also needs to be a coolhunter.**
> This symbiotic relationship between coolfarmer Mark Hunter and Cory Kennedy has turned out to be highly beneficial to both of them, turning Cory into a celebrity, while also greatly increasing Mark's standing as a photographer and celebrity launcher. Great coolfarming from both sides.

For another example of a coolfarmer who is also a stellar coolhunter, look at Oprah Winfrey. Talk show master Oprah has become one of the richest people in America by being a big discoverer and developer of talent. When she hunts for cool books to be featured in her book club, there is almost inevitably an explosion of sales numbers for any author lucky enough to make it into her club. But this only works because there is absolutely nothing in it for her selling the author's books. She does not take a cut from the books. Her only objective is—at least for this book-club venture—the altruistic goal of bettering society by getting millions of Americans to read a good book, instead of slouching in front of the TV watching a football game or soap opera.

How Do Leaders Get Selected?

Now that we know that great coolfarmers are also great coolhunters, the question is: Who is coolhunting for the leaders of the swarm, and who is coolfarming them? Linus Torvalds gives an excellent description on how other leaders in the Linux kernel team are selected. As he described it in an interview, ". . . [L]ieutenants get picked. It's not me or any other leader who picks them. The programmers are very good at selecting leaders. There is no process for making somebody a lieutenant. But somebody who gets things done, shows good taste, and has good qualities—people just start sending them suggestions and software updates. I didn't design it this way. This happens because this is the way people work. It's very natural."[15]

COOLFARMING LESSON: COIN leaders are chosen by the swarm.

It is not the leader, then, who chooses the people working with him, but the members of the swarm who choose the leader who is best for them. They make their choice based on the skills and personality of the leader. Anchored in the reputation of the leaders, their royal pheromone, people select other people with whom to collaborate. They are proud of the goals of the leader and, foremost, of themselves working for the goals. People working with Nicholas Negroponte on the OLPC, with Linus Torvalds on Linux, and with Tim Berners-Lee on the Web have chosen to work with them because they believe in the goals and the vision of the leader, and they also believe that the leader can take them there. Every COIN member is both coolfarmer and coolhunter, continuously looking for cool ideas and people.

There are some other tangible things one can do to become a creator. None of them is easy, but in combination, they make up key success factors of winning creators. To understand them better, we travel again to Ghana, looking at how—against all odds—some amazing coolfarmers succeeded there, in the middle of Africa.

Coolfarming Tourists—Immersing Yourself into the Swarm

I met Jonas when I was staying at the beach resort of Axim (Figure 3–2), in the western part of the Ghanaian coast, near the Ivory Coast border. Jonas, the owner of the resort, told me his incredible story.

Jonas got his first taste of tourism as a twenty-one-year-old touring the world. After a childhood spent in Ghana and the United Kingdom, he traveled as a backpacker in Asia, visiting China, Thailand, and Hong Kong. When he was staying in a youth hostel in Hong Kong he ran out of money. He asked the hostel owner for a loan and the owner offered him a job instead, running the night shift of a second hostel he also owned in Hong Kong. Jonas liked this job so much that he decided to start a tourism business back in his native Ghana. On the same trip to Southeast Asia, he also met his future German wife. Falling in love caused him to make a multiyear

FIGURE 3-2. Axim beach resort in Ghana.

detour to Germany, but three years later, together with a German friend, they toured all of Ghana, looking for the most beautiful spot to start a hotel. When they discovered the beaches of Axim, they immediately fell in love with the place. Equipped with three bottles of schnapps, they visited the local chieftain. When he heard their idea, he was very supportive and let them have the land. The first thing the two tourism entrepreneurs had to do was to build an access road to the beach and clear the land of the many snakes that had been the main inhabitants until then. Over the next nineteen years, Jonas and his partners built a dozen small cottages, "chalets" as they call them, in the native style and provided about forty jobs in this country where the mouths to feed are many, and jobs are scarce.

I first met Jonas when I was sitting one windy evening in the restaurant of the beach resort with my children, eating an excellent fish meal. The fish was getting cold rapidly, because the wind was so strong. Suddenly, somebody asked if he could lower the wind shades for me, and then quickly proceeded to put down some wind screens. Only when the waiters rushed to help him did I take second notice of the man. Obviously he was somebody people cared about at this resort. After a quick conversation, it became clear that he was the owner of this beautiful resort situated on a romantic hill overlooking the Atlantic coast of Ghana.

As a guest in one of Jonas's cottages, I was surprised to learn that the shower actually gave hot water, the cottages were equipped with working air conditioners, there was electricity around the clock, and all—well, most—of the items on the menu were actually available. Best of all, to generate the hot water for the showers, Jonas had imported solar-powered water heaters. He also had set up a satellite dish to operate an Internet café, and had become an avid Internet user himself.

Sipping a beer in his restaurant, Jonas explained his philosophy to me. "In the beginning, it was not easy," he said. "The local people claimed that we had killed a worker and buried him behind the cottages. Fortunately, the relationship has now entirely changed. I am supporting the local hospital and the elementary and secondary schools, and we have also financed street lighting in the Axim main street. Now the relationship with the local community is excellent, and we are recognized as one of the main employers in the tourism sector." His cottages are built using local construction technologies, with adobe bricks and loam. Jonas learned about advanced loam construction in Germany and applied his insights to his chalets to improve the native designs.

Jonas is a successful coolfarmer. Early on, he decided that he would cater to backpackers and individual tourists who like a quiet place built in genuinely indigenous style. As Jonas had been part of this swarm himself as a backpacker in Asia, he knew his target group extremely well and was able to customize his resort to their tastes, which were also his. He was employing simple but functional native designs and construction technologies. The effect is stunning: The chalets and the restaurant, even down to the details of the umbrellas, are all built in the local style, only with much more durable materials, and equipped with electricity.

As a former backpacker, Jonas is continuously listening to the swarm. He knew this group is quite price-sensitive, but also likes well-functioning and well-equipped accommodations. His cottages are not fancy, but they are very solidly built and come with satellite TV and a working bathroom, including a hot shower—which is definitively exceptional in Ghana. Initially Jonas did not have air-conditioning in his cottages, but his customers, many of them Western expatriates in Ghana, told him that they would be willing to pay slightly more if the cottages were cooled. Jonas was happy to oblige, and on my last visit I found that all cottages now have air-conditioning. Although Jonas raised the price per night by five dollars, all cottages were still sold out while I was there.

Jonas immerses himself into both the tourist swarm as well as the swarm of his own employees. He is residing in one of his own cottages, as his own customer. He also takes his meals in his own restaurants and uses every occasion to talk with his customers. On the other hand, he takes every opportunity to work with his employees. He was a construction worker in Germany and participated as a worker in the building of his cottages. His guiding principle is to understand all tasks and activities needed in his hotel. He has sampled every item on his menu list. When I told him that my children did not really like the pizza that his chef made, he told me that he had noticed the same thing, and that he had already arranged for a German(!) expert pizza maker to come train his chef to produce real pizza dough. He also trains his employees to continuously ask the guests for feedback. Whenever I entered the office, the staff there would ask for my opinion about how they could improve my experience at the resort.

At the same time Jonas is also sharing with the swarm. Jonas told me that he pays his employees very well, which allows him to pick his staff from the large group of well-trained people from Accra. He offers them nice lodging facilities, too—in fact, the employee housing is of such high quality that unoccupied staff rooms are rented out to tourists as overflow accommodation if all the cottages are sold out. This is quite in contrast to other Ghanaian hotels, where employees live in slums outside the hotel. Jonas also is on excellent terms with the local community of Axim. He is a large employer of local construction workers, as he is continuously renovating and extending his cottages. He is popular with local schools as a benefactor and donor of teaching materials. He provided his technical expertise to connect the local hospital to the Internet and to equip downtown Axim with street lighting.

As the queen bee of his swarm of cooks, maids, and houseboys, Jonas demands a lot—from others and most of all from himself. For a long time Jonas held two jobs, because while he was managing his resort hotel he was also financing construction of the resort by working as a construction worker part of the year in Germany. When I met him most recently, he had finally given up on his foreign work and was focusing his full energy on improving his resort. In contrast to many other places in Ghana where hotel customer service is seriously lacking, his staff was courteous and focused on fulfilling all my wishes. Jonas told me that he introduced the concept of the employee of the year, and this year his best worker was the hotel boy whose task is manually mowing the grass with a cutlass and carrying the suitcases of hotel guests to the cottages.

Of course, his staff also knows that Jonas will be breathing down their necks if they don't perform, because Jonas is a perfectionist. He chose to have the best two-star lodge in Ghana, instead of yet another three- or four-star hotel. In his quest to make guests feel truly welcome in their cottages, he makes sure that little flowers are liberally sprinkled all across the bedrooms, in the bathroom, and on the tables. The sheets on the beds are not just folded squarely, but are neatly arranged as little pieces of art, together with a few pretty flowers. The walls in the bathrooms are plastered with beautifully laid-out patterns made from real clamshells. Because red dust is everywhere in Ghana, Jonas has some construction workers on permanent staffing to continuously repair and repaint the cottages to give them their fresh look.

Jonas is not afraid to stray from conventional wisdom, either, and voice a different opinion. Frequently he has blazed new trails. He was first to set up an Internet café far way from central Accra. Jonas is also very much ahead of the rest of Ghana with his focus on sustainable energy sources. Environmental and green technologies are not popular in Ghana's emerging economy, and there is talk of supplementing the Volta power plant with a nuclear power plant. Jonas, however, besides installing solar energy–powered water heaters, is also equipping the first cottages with geothermic air conditioners drawing their energy from deep earth probes, which he imports from Germany.

> **COOLFARMING LESSON: Creators immerse themselves into their swarm.**
>
> By immersing himself into different swarms, initially touring the world as a backpacker, then later being both a member of the tourist swarm and the worker swarm in his own resort, Jonas is a living, breathing success story, with one of the most famous beach resorts whose reputation extends far beyond Ghana.

Coolfarming a Palm Tree Plantation— Empowering the Community

My introduction to Jonas happened through another notable cool-farmer, Kwame. Returning from Switzerland with his savings as a guest worker there for ten years, Kwame started an oil palm tree plantation in Ghana four years before I met him. On about 100 hectares of land he planted 19,000 palm trees. This palm tree plantation is complemented by a pig barn, a duck pond, and stables for goats and chickens. Of course, he could not do all this farming by himself, but needed lots of help. The most labor-intensive work is planting new palm tree saplings and tending to the growing saplings. He initially hired about twenty-five workers from nearby villages to take care of the trees, plus some others to tend to the pigs, goats, and ducks. The workers' task was to remove the weeds around the young trees, apply fertilizer, and chase away pests such as tree-eating insects and rodents.

On the last workday of the first month of operation, Kwame paid each worker his agreed-on monthly salary in cash, as is the custom in

Ghana. On the next working day, he was in for a bad surprise. Out of his twenty-five workers, only four showed up. The others, they said, did not want to come this month because they now had enough money to get by for the next month; some of them might come back to the farm perhaps in a month or two, when they would need money again. This was, of course, not a good situation—in a month or two the young palm trees would all be overgrown by the weeds and eaten by the insects and rodents.

To overcome this problem, my friend Kwame came up with a brilliant idea. Instead of hiring workers, he decided to hire communities. He does not pay them per day, but for tasks. When I was visiting, he had hired one village to weed 600 palm trees. He negotiated a price with the elders of the village for this task, and now it was up to the villagers to make sure that the work was done. The community needed the money to pay for poles to get electricity to the village. If a lazy villager did not show up for work, the community would force him to pay a fine. During my entire visit at the farm, the group of villagers was hard at work weeding the 600 palm trees, cutting down the weeds with their cutlasses. Kwame told me that he had made similar agreements with other villages to get all of his 19,000 trees weeded.

> **COOLFARMING LESSON: Creators empower the community.**
> By giving away power to the community, letting the workers manage themselves, Kwame was able to obtain the necessary care for his palm trees. Relying on self-organizing communities, my friend had overcome the mindset of the villagers, solving his problem of tending to his oil palms not by hiring workers, but by unleashing the power of swarms. To gain power, one needs to give away power.

Running an Internet Café in Ghana— Using the Swarm to Police the Swarm

When flying in to Accra on one of my trips to Ghana, I started a discussion with my neighbor on the plane. When I had told him about my project of trying to set up an Internet café for a school in a fishermen's village on the coast of Ghana, he told me that he was running one of the largest Internet cafés in Ghana.

The next morning we went to see his Internet café, a bustling place in the business district of Accra. The entrance to the building led to a large room equipped with fifty computers. In the back of the room there was a printing and copying center, and private rooms to be rented for videoconferencing. Outside the building a large power generator was droning along, because the public electricity grid in Ghana is very unreliable. As a good businessman, my new friend Tom had set up a few chairs and tables outside and was also selling ice cream, to put his reliable energy system to a second use powering a steadily cooled ice-box. During our brief visit, both the computers inside and the chairs outside were always at least two-thirds occupied—it seems that the Internet and ice cream have obtained a firm place in Ghanaian life.

We then started talking some more, and Tom told me some stories about how he managed his Internet café. These stories once more illustrate how swarm creativity empowers collaborative innovation.

When he had first come to Ghana from America, planning to open a business in Ghana, he had hired a taxi driver to take him around and hunt for a business opportunity. Although he failed to find the opportunity he was looking for, he struck up a friendship with his cab driver. In the end, Tom, his taxi driver, and a friend of the taxi driver decided to start the Internet café. Tom's Internet café is now thriving, employing about twenty-five people. He runs his café twenty-four hours a day, seven days a week, with three shifts of employees. His staff is quite knowledgeable, even developing proprietary cybercafé management software. The venue also has a reputation for high availability and reliability in a country where the infrastructure breaks down frequently. It uses the latest computer hardware, not secondhand computers donated from the West, and has high-speed access, making it a favorite among local businesses and tourists.

Tom knows that to be part of the swarm, he needs to share with the swarm. On Saturdays, he opens the doors of his Internet café for free to the children of a local middle school. In collaboration with a computer science professor of a local university, Tom is offering training to the children. The Internet café provides the infrastructure, and the university provides the tutors. Every Saturday morning, university computer science students come teach the kids computer basics. Of course, this is a "give and take" investment, because some of the kids might return later on as customers, or even as potential employees.

The power of the swarm can also be used to police the swarm and weed out the drones.

While the Internet café was doing very well, with computers fully occupied most of the time, Tom started noticing that revenues were declining. Suspecting foul play, he had to enlist the help of the swarm to remove the rotten apples.

In one incident, the cash revenues seemed to go down. Assuming theft by employees, he began to investigate. To find the potential culprit, Tom decided to put web technology to productive use. He asked his technical staff to set up a web camera and a motion sensor focused on the cash register to catch the thief. It turned out that the money was being stolen by one of the shift managers. He was clearly caught, on the digital recording, sticking his hand into the cash register and helping himself to a generous handful of cash in the quiet night hours. Remarkably, the technical staff member who had installed the camera did not give the trap away to his fellow employees at the company.

The bee in this case was sticking with the bee queen, and not with the other bees of the hive. Of course, with bee logic, this makes perfect sense, as the thieving employee was behaving not as a bee, but as a drone, stealing honey from the swarm. And as we know by now, at some point drones are kicked out by the swarm.

Tom also told me of a second incident where the bees once again stuck with the queen. One of the managers at the café had a physical handicap and had to come to work every morning by taxi, with the company paying his fare. Tom was devastated to discover that the same employee had seriously misappropriated funds by giving himself large cash advances. At first he was at a loss what to do. The individual embezzling the money was one of his most senior employees who, until now, had had his full trust. Because the café had done well, financially, this year, Tom had planned to give all employees a year-end bonus. This was now at risk. So Tom called an all-hands meeting of his employees. At this meeting, things first started going badly when the man embezzling the money acted rebellious, obviously trying to plant the seeds of a revolt against Tom among the other employees.

In the end, Tom decided to employ the power of the swarm and turn the swarm against the drone. He told his employees that the planned bonus they all were hoping to get now most likely could not be paid. One employee had been giving himself large cash advances against the monthly revenues of the entire business, leaving no money for the year-end bonuses. This was enough for the other employees to turn against this senior manager, siding with Tom and asking the other manager to return the embezzled money. While Tom did not get much money back—it was already spent—he got back the goodwill, the loyalty, and the cooperation of his swarm. By operating with transparency and sharing the accounting numbers with his staff members, Tom made it clear to all employees that the actions of one bad apple meant that they might not be getting a bonus. This also meant that the thief had little success in staging his planned revolt against Tom.

> **COOLFARMING LESSON: Creators share with the swarm.**
> In both cases, one involving an employee taking the money from the cash register and the other a senior manager embezzling money, the swarm was policing the swarm. This was only possible because Tom was also sharing with the swarm, by having a revenue-sharing program in place, and by offering free Internet training to local schoolchildren on Saturday mornings, thus acquiring goodwill from both his employees and the local community.

Seven Guidelines for Creators

Based on the coolfarming lessons from Ghana, here are some rules to consider for your own coolfarming. While they are not the only recipe for diffusing the royal pheromone and being fed the royal jelly, they certainly are helpful for getting the buy-in of the swarm.

1. Choose your swarm. Decide who will be the target group for your cool innovation. Not all the same people find the same idea cool. Former backpacker Jonas, the tourism entrepreneur in Ghana, decided to cater to the swarm of backpackers he knew best from his own experience. While he also set up an Internet café at his hotel in Axim, it was mostly as a service for tourists, so it markedly differed from the business that my friend, Tom, the Internet café entrepreneur, created to cater to the Internet needs of the local business community in Ghana.

2. Listen to the swarm. Embed and tailor your vision and message according to the needs and wishes of your target group. Jonas, the resort owner, is constantly listening to and serving the wishes of his customers, as demonstrated when he personally lowered the shades at my table in the outdoor restaurant when he thought it would be too windy.

3. Immerse yourself into the swarm. Become a seamless part of the swarm, and don't expect preferential treatment. Jonas has performed all the jobs at his resort: He works in the rooms, he helps his construction workers to build new guesthouses, he works in the kitchen and in reception. The same is true for successful coolfarmer Kwame, who, at my last visit, was weeding the palm trees with a cutlass together with his teams of workers.

4. Share with the swarm. Give back the profits you make from the work of the swarm, and share fame, glory, and revenue with all members of the swarm. As an equally important auxiliary, always give credit to anyone who deserves credit! Tom, the Internet café owner in Ghana, was only able to turn back a planned revolt by his number-two manager because he had the loyalty of the rest of the employees, who all participated in the profits of the Internet café in a revenue-sharing plan. At Jonas's resort, I experienced for myself the excellent service of the motivated houseboy carrying my bags to the cabin, who was publicly recognized as one of the most valuable members of the staff.

5. Demand a lot—from others and, most of all, from yourself. Coolfarmer Kwame is the first worker on his palm tree farm in the morning, camping out in a newly built farmhouse without running water and electricity, mostly living off cornflakes prepared with hot water, powdered milk, and sugar. As a kid from the city, he is learning about raising pigs from the veterinarian he has hired, and about weeding the palm trees from the local farmers.

6. Be a perfectionist. According to Aristotle's *Ethics:* "The shoemaker should strive to build the best possible pair of shoes with the leather he has available." Jonas chose to have the best two-star lodge, instead of another also-ran three-star hotel. He demands that little flowers be placed in the bathrooms and on the table. The sheets are folded as little pieces of art. This way, he offers a unique presentation to his guests. When I did an informal poll on my second visit, most of the guests in the sold-out resort were repeat customers.

7. *Don't be afraid to have a different opinion.* Successful coolfarmers are walking outside the well-trodden paths. Jonas provides hot water to hotel guests using sustainable energy sources. Kwame is investing in pig breeding in a country where rice, fish, goat, and chicken are mainstays of the diet. My friend the Internet café owner is investing in high-speed satellite connections and the latest computer hardware while his competitors rely on unreliable landline connections and used computers. All of these coolfarmers defy conventional wisdom, with stellar results.

The next chapter looks at the next phase, where a group of people sharing the same vision find each other. The team comes together in a COIN—a Collaborative Innovation Network—to take up the ideas of the creator, turning them into a real product.

4

COINs
Building the Product

Fluctuat nec mergitur: "It shakes, but it does not sink."

MEMBERS OF A COIN are intrinsically motivated to reach the shared goal—be it to develop a new type of lightweight mountain bike or the next version of an open-source computer program. They decide for themselves when they want to do what, because they are passionate about the vision, goals, and results of their collaborative effort, and not because they are ordered or paid to do it.

In a COIN, people think like a swarm. They communicate their thoughts and ideas to each other and then figure out the rights or wrongs together. They don't follow rules and regulations that tell them what they should or should not do. Rather, they make the rules *by themselves, for themselves.* As the COIN expands its knowledge and skills, each individual member also grows in skills, knowledge, and personal maturity. An individual's success is realized through the success of the COIN, because the goal of the COIN is the goal of each COIN member.

Combining the collective intelligence of experts in a COIN leads to a group whose wisdom vastly exceeds the sum of individual expertise. Most experts think that they know the answer in their field of expertise. This is not necessarily true, however. Each expert often only knows part of the answer. The individual expert's solution might have solved the problem in the past, but this does not mean that there are not better ways to solve the same problem. Only by creatively combining the solutions of multiple experts, by forcing different theories and approaches to be tested by the others, can we get the best answer. The idea is to try to get different expert opinions and ideally expose your experts to the different recommendations of their colleagues.

> *COOLFARMING LESSON: COINs develop disruptive innovation.*
>
> This way of thinking usually does not go over well with old-school companies. Traditional companies don't like disruptive change; they like to carefully map out their progress in five-year and ten-year plans. Therefore their innovations will be transformative; that is, they'll refine and improve on the "old" ways—how things have always been done. On the other hand, COINs question conventional wisdom, so innovations from COINs might even cannibalize existing product lines of the company. If, as a group, a COIN works well, its output will be of superior quality, beating by far the output of groups managed by conventional project management principles of command and control.

To better understand the important things that COINs can achieve, let's look at a COIN started by a truly amazing man.

How Picasso Created Cubism Through a COIN

Pablo Picasso was a creator, coolhunter, and coolfarmer. He undoubtedly is one of the most creative artists ever, not only as a painter, but also as a sculptor and potter. Like any great coolfarmer, he reinvented himself and his art numerous times, being instrumental in creating new styles of art—most famously Cubism—not on his own, but together with a COIN.

Picasso was lucky to be born the son of an art professor, who early on recognized the unusual talent of his son and supported and nurtured him through his early youth and adolescence. But in puberty Picasso's rebellious streak caused him to break with his father. The father had succeeded in getting his precocious son into the art academy in Madrid, the most famous and highly respected training school in Spain for aspiring artists. But instead of attending school, Picasso stayed home in the room his father had rented for him, and he painted. Soon thereafter he left Madrid and moved to Paris.

Picasso went through different phases, starting with the Blue Period, drawing in the postimpressionist styles of Paul Gauguin, Edgar Degas, and Henri de Toulouse-Lautrec. His paintings in this period were mostly expressing human misery, portraying beggars, alcoholics, prostitutes, and poor children with their long drawn-out elongated limbs reminiscent of Spanish Renaissance painter El Greco. While undoubtedly a genius and painting in his own style, Picasso in this phase was standing on the shoulders of these earlier artistic giants.

After the Blue Period came the Rose Period. In a happy relationship with girlfriend and muse Fernande Olivier, Picasso started painting more cheerful subjects in shades of rose and pink. When drawing a harlequin, he was representing his own self at that time. In this phase, during 1904 and 1905, Picasso also struck up friendships with other influential artists such as poet Max Jacob, writers Guillaume Apollinaire and Gertrude Stein, as well as art dealers Ambroise Vollard and Daniel-Henry Kahnweiler. Picasso was building his first COIN, Collaborative Learning Network, and Collaborative Interest Network all at the same time.

The Rose Period led to Picasso's most famous innovation, Cubism. His painting *Les Demoiselles d'Avignon* (1907), showing a group of nude women in an abstract triangular style, was so radical that in the beginning he did not even dare show it to his friends. In 1908, the small COIN of painters who later on became famous as the founders of Cubism began to take shape, more consistently applying the style pioneered by Picasso in *Les Demoiselles d'Avignon*. Picasso, together with French painter Georges Braque, started experimenting with this radically new way of reducing all objects to cubes—hence the name "Cubism." This name, by the way, was not invented by either Picasso or Braque, but was quickly adopted by the two when they heard their style labeled this way for the first time.

Picasso mostly painted landscapes, but also musical instruments, still-life objects, and portraits of his friends. The first Cubism COIN consisted only of Picasso and Braque, but they were soon joined by Spanish painter Juan Gris. Very quickly, the COIN recruited new members, mostly artists working in close proximity in the Montmartre quarter in Paris. Robert Delaunay, Marcel Duchamp and his brothers Raymond Duchamp-Villon and Jacques Villon, Fernand Léger, and Francis Picabia became important representatives of the Cubist art movement. They in fact created an offshoot of Cubism named for the suburb of Puteaux where they were based. They first formed a Collaborative Learning Network or CLN, later on growing into their own COIN. Besides the Puteaux Group, which included dozens of members, there were other peripheral members of the Cubism COIN who either joined the core COIN or started their own artistic offspring.

The way Pablo Picasso and Georges Braque created Cubism again demonstrates the core traits of creators and COIN members. Setting out with no concrete plan of action, but armed with a great vision and through sheer force of will, they succeeded against all the odds. And the odds were high in those years. Picasso was so poor he sometimes had to burn his own paintings in the stove in his bedroom in Paris just to heat his room.

A COIN goes through multiple phases. Just like Picasso went through the Blue and Rose periods to discover Cubism, COINs continually experiment with different ideas, picking up inspirations from the most unlikely sources.

COIN members are great networkers. On their continuous and never-ending journey toward their grand vision, they pick up—and occasionally shed—a great number of friends and collaborators. Just like Picasso teamed up with poets, writers, and art dealers, COIN members reach out to people outside their core domain for help. But at the same time, just like Picasso teamed up with Braque and Gris, COIN members are renowned for getting together in a core team with other birds of a feather—the like-minded souls brave enough to join them in venturing out into new, uncharted territory.

COOLFARMING LESSON: COINs go through multiple phases. The product of a COIN draws from, but also influences, related fields. The ideas of Cubism flowed over into other fields, such as writing and poetry. For example, poets such as Guillaume Apollinaire, Blaise Cendrars, Jean Cocteau, and Max Jacob became important representatives of the Cubist style of writing. This mutual cross-fertilization between COINs is true not just for art, but for any COIN-driven innovative work.

After learning about the basic principles of COINs in the art world, let's now look at how they are applied in business.

Gain Power by Giving It Up— Rotating Leadership

Apple and Google know that the key to innovation is collaboration. That's why Apple's iPhone shows lots of Google Maps, and why the two high-tech giants teamed up to develop a battery-saving video player for the iPhone to play back Google's YouTube videos. Why does this collaboration work so well for Google and Apple?

Professors Jason Davis from MIT and Kathleen Eisenhardt from Stanford University studied eight collaboratively developed high-tech products, where two companies teamed up to develop something fundamentally new. Inspired by products like the Motorola Razr, Apple's iPhone, and Microsoft's Xbox, Davis and Eisenhardt were looking for the secrets of successful collaboration among team members coming from different companies.

The eight collaboratively developed projects all consisted mostly of software. The products included security firmware, middleware, mobile e-mail applications, and Internet telephony hardware and software. The collaborating firms were almost evenly headquartered inside and outside of the United States. Most of the companies had previous relationships as buyers, suppliers, or direct competitors. The researchers factored into their analysis how well the collaborating companies were already connected with their partners and other peers in the industry.

In conducting many interviews over two years, Davis and Eisenhardt focused on the organizational processes steering the mode of collaboration. The people they interviewed were well aware of the advantages of collaboration. For example, one CTO said, "If you want to study innovation in my industry, you need to study

collaboration. . . . In fact, you'd be hard-pressed to find a single innovative product that isn't the result of specific, strategic technology collaborations. Honestly, I spend 80 percent of my time doing
collaborations. That's how important it is."[2]

The success of the collaboration was measured by the number of
new technologies created, new patents and other intellectual property
developed, and new products brought to market. The researchers
complemented these quantitative measures by asking the interviewees
about their perception of the success of the collaboration.

Davis and Eisenhardt found some important examples of teams
where collaboration works, and where it does not. The high-
performing teams very much worked as COINs. But even highly
successful collaborations like the one between Microsoft and Intel
can be fraught with rifts along the way. Highly creative work frequently looks chaotic from the outside. And indeed, COINs are
shaken by waves of creativity. Managing a creative process is a
chaotic process in itself.

FLUCTUATING CONTROL

The most productive projects were the ones where project ownership went back and forth between the two partnering companies.
This means that neither domineering leadership nor a consensus-
building approach worked best. In the best teams, control of the
project fluctuated between the two partner companies. Even if the
two companies were of vastly different sizes, it was important that
at different points on the progress line toward completion of the
product, decision-making power lay with one of the two companies
at any given point in time. In order to gain power, one needs to give
up power. Occasionally, Goliath needs to transfer power to David,
and the other way around. In fact, Davis and Eisenhardt noted that
a manager at one joint project said, "I really don't know who I am
working for now. Most of my time is spent at their headquarters

trying to implement their strategy with my firm's resources. It's confusing."[3] This type of collaboration is not always easy. Which firm will be filing for what patents? Who will own which intellectual property?

Firms that were successful had very clear responsibilities. For example, members of firm A said they would let firm B control the deadlines, only to take over these responsibilities in the next phase when firm B was facing external problems. Once firm B's crisis was resolved, it returned to take on project leadership for the following phase.

This revolving decision control allowed the two firms to capitalize on each other's expertise. It also allowed them to make some unexpected combinations of their complementary technology and expertise. In one example, combining firm A's expertise on open source and Linux with firm B's knowledge of virtual private networks allowed mobile users to access data securely in ways neither of the two firms had thought of before. In another illustration of the advantages of rotational leadership, firm A's experience in open-source projects allowed firm B to use firm A's community of developers to test early versions of their new virtual private network. As one of firm A's managers told the researchers, "We don't just want an enabling program. We want them [firm B] as a co-creator of [the new technology] and that means making them heavily involved. . . ."[4]

Domineering leadership arrangements demotivated the dominated partners, causing them to withhold their most relevant knowledge. But consensus-leadership approaches also were less than optimal. Sharing control in every phase with joint strategic decision making led to deep misunderstandings on both sides, which tended to be kept under the table until it was too late. Despite extensive discussions, both project partners had widely differing views on important issues, leading to mutual finger-pointing and significant project delays.

CHANGING OUTSIDE PARTNERS

A second key finding by professors Davis and Eisenhardt was that the network of external partners changed a lot along the way to project completion. Usually, the company that was in charge at any given point in time would bring in its own external partners first. When control switched to the other company, that company then would bring in its own preferred external partners.

This way, the project members from both companies could tap into a much wider active network of external partners. Professors Davis and Eisenhardt liken this process to a waterfall whose source shifts over time with a fluctuating cascade of participants, where different people are involved in the same activities at different phases of the project. For example, Linux open-source firm A was able to get access to security networking engineers through the CTO of networking firm B early on. Later in the process, Linux firm A was able to collaborate with other engineers at security networking firm B through the same executive sponsor at the security networking firm.

This mode of operation was very different from projects operating in the domineering partnership model. There, the dominant partner would keep project team membership stable over the course of the project, thus limiting access to crucial knowledge, which was available inside the domineering firm but not accessible to the smaller project partner. Consensus leadership, on the other hand, ensured maximum involvement of project team members from both sides, but also involved high coordination costs and seemed to tire participants over time.

CHANGING STRATEGY ALONG THE WAY

The professors further noticed a zigzag of strategy shifts and changes along the way. The changes in project ownership also brought changes in product strategy. Through rotating leadership, the project was able to much more flexibly adapt to external changes. These changes also permitted much broader searches for new innovations to be integrated into the new product, leading to a higher-quality product. For example, company A was an adherent of the open-source strategy, while company B derived its revenue through licensing its proprietary software. As a consequence of rotational leadership, parts of the newly developed software were developed under open source, while other parts were patented and codified as trade secrets. However, over the course of the project, company B came to discover the advantages of open source, leading it to pursue a more open intellectual property strategy.

The impact of rotating leadership was striking in some cases; in fits and starts, product development moved down zigzagging development paths that were impossible to predict, exploring new ideas in ways that neither of the partners could have done on its own. Each zigzag allowed the leading firm to reach its strategic objective and the non-leading firm to better understand these objectives.

By contrast, the domineering collaboration strategy was much more susceptible to unforeseen roadblocks in trying to follow the original project plan laid out by the domineering partner. Consensus leadership was less productive also, as too much effort was wasted on obtaining agreement on minor issues instead of focusing on innovation.

THE BENEFITS OF ROTATING LEADERSHIP

While the rotational leadership approach also carries uncertainties and risks, and can lead to anxiety for team members, the benefits far outweigh these possible disadvantages. Organizations collaborating in a symbiotic relationship under the rotational leadership model are superior in handling ambiguous situations with unpredictable outcomes. Another advantage was that, at every phase in the project, responsibilities were quite clear, but could be redefined in the next phase by rotating the leadership if need be.

This model is far more efficient than a rigid hierarchy fixed for the lifetime of the COIN, or an egalitarian approach where each disagreement is put on the table and discussed at great length. COINs are not egalitarian, but meritocratic. This means that in COINs, while leadership roles can always be questioned, they are clear at any given point in time.

> **COOLFARMING LESSON: COINs have leaders, but rotating leadership.**
> The willingness of COIN leaders to give up their leadership posts opens the way to integrating new ideas through bringing in fresh blood at any given point in time. Having clear leaders means that there are always individuals who will feel empowered and will demonstrate a high level of commitment.

Start Out as a Small Fish in a Big Pond

What is the best way for a COIN to launch and market its new ideas? A team of analysts studying cancer research in France looked at what distinguished the most successful cancer researchers from their less successful peers. Analyzing which researchers got their ideas disseminated the fastest, they found that it paid for junior researchers to be a "small fish in a big pond."[5]

The analysts looked at the senior researchers at French government-sponsored and private research centers and university labs. They separated the researchers into four categories:

- "Big Fish in the Big Ponds" were the most senior and successful researchers, mostly lab directors, group leaders, and university professors working at large and prestigious research labs.

- "Big Fish in the Little Ponds" were the well-respected researchers working at small and less famous institutions.

❑ "Small Fish in the Big Ponds" were less influential junior researchers at large and prestigious research labs.

❑ "Small Fish in the Little Ponds" were the less influential people working at small institutions.

When comparing and measuring the success among these four categories of researchers, they found that researchers, even the "small fish," working in a big pond (i.e., located at a large and well-respected institution) had much greater impact than researchers working at small institutions, even the "big fish." So, although it might be nicer for the ego of a "small fish" to work at a provincial institution, where a researcher might find it easier to have local impact, the global impact of these researchers was very low. Small fish got much more recognition if they worked at a prestigious institution. It seems that the shadow of the big fish at the prestigious institutions did not hinder progress of the small fish in the same organizations. Quite the opposite. Small fish profited from the aura of the big fish at their institution.

In a second experiment, the researchers studied over a five-year period the strategies of the small fish who successfully became big fish. Toward that goal, they distinguished between four strategies of collaboration employed by the different researchers. They grouped the different collaboration strategies by looking at how much a researcher was asked for advice by others, and how much the researcher asked others for advice.

❑ People in the first group were the individualist researchers who worked entirely independent from others. These researchers neither asked for advice, nor were they asked.

❑ The second category of researchers included those who were not regularly asked for advice by others, but who frequently asked others for advice.

❏ The third category consisted of the researchers who provided advice, but did not ask others for advice.

❏ Researchers in the fourth group were the most social ones; they not only freely shared advice, but also frequently went out to get advice from others.

What the researchers found is that it pays to give and take advice. Not surprisingly, the most social researchers, who both gave and asked for advice frequently, were the most successful in becoming big fish themselves. The individualist researchers, on the other hand, who neither gave nor asked for advice, were the most likely to remain little fish forever. Researchers who either asked for advice or gave advice, but not both, were in the middle category. For them, if given the choice to either use their time to give advice or ask for advice, it turned out that the researchers giving advice were more likely to become big fish than the ones focusing on asking for advice.

COOLFARMING LESSON: Tell others what you know.
One can never communicate enough. Researchers who choose to lock themselves in a chamber in the ivory tower of science have a much harder time succeeding than the ones who reach out to their colleagues by networking at conferences, continuously learning from others and teaching others. The best predictor of future success seems to be the teaching activities of the researchers. Willingness to take the time to give advice to others, to tell others what one knows, is good not only for the advice-seeker, but also for the advice-giver.

The conclusion seems obvious—it pays to be altruistic and help others advance in their careers, because in return they will also help you to become a big fish in a big pond!

Six Guidelines for COINs

1. Waggle dance for the best honeybees. The most successful COINs are those that recruit the best and most highly respected members. Creators—while continuing to do their waggle dance—should strive only for the best, even if the process of reaching their goal might take much more time that way.

2. Understand that COIN members work for the greater good and an ego boost. The main motivation for people to join a COIN is to contribute to a shared goal about which they are passionate, not to make money or get famous. These two motivations, in this order—first for the greater good, to make the world a better place in some way, and second for some ego boosting—are the main reasons that people join a COIN.

3. Allow COINs to go through multiple phases. Picasso went through his Blue and Red periods to discover Cubism. COINs go through many different phases, with differing membership and different tactical goals, without losing sight of the big vision, of course.

4. Accept rotational leadership. The most successful innovation teams at collaborating high-tech companies rotate leadership. In COINs, too, at any given phase, there is a clear leader, but the leader is willing to pass on leadership to whoever is the most capable of reaching the goal for the next phase.

5. Be a small fish in a big pond. French researchers found that junior cancer researchers succeed more rapidly working from prestigious research labs. In the same vein, it is better for the goals of a COIN to be associated with a powerful incubating environment. COINs should associate themselves with and draw inspiration from successful organizations. Look at Steve Jobs, who got his ideas for Apple Computer from the famous Xerox Palo Alto Research Center

(PARC), or Google, which was started by two students from Stanford, one of the top U.S. universities.

6. Ask and give advice. The French cancer researchers documented the benefits of engaging in a mutual dialogue of giving and receiving help. Selflessness and altruism are not just good for the environment, but also for the people sharing what they know.

This in-depth discussion of how to nurture and foster collaboration to create the product at the core of the COIN leads us to the next chapter, on how COIN members leverage their friends and family network to both learn about best uses and potential enhancements for their product *and* recruit new members for their COIN.

5

CLNs
Teaching and Preaching the Gospel

Docendo discimus: "We learn by teaching."

WHEN THE BEE swarm sends out coolhunters looking for a new home, the scouts are searching for the new hive location with the best attributes. The same is true for human coolfarmers. Once they have signed on to the vision and goals of their swarm, they will be working to increase acceptance of their visionary new product.

This is the phase where the COIN members need to find out what works best to make their product attractive to their community. Toward that goal, they tap into their network of friends and family, their Collaborative Learning Network (CLN). The CLN is both an invaluable sounding board for the daring new ideas of the COIN and a fertile source of new COIN members. CLN members will be the first ones to try out the evolving product of the COIN. If the COIN members do their waggle dance well, they will also motivate some of the people from the CLN to increase their level of commitment, to join the core COIN.

For example, the owners of a small brewery in Denmark open-sourced their recipe for beer. Teaching others how to make their own beer in the end proved highly beneficial to the inventors of the original recipe. Publishing their "Freebeer" recipe, they let the swarm define the attributes of their product. The open-sourced beer recipe encouraged beer fanatics from all around the world to test it out. Some of these beer lovers started brewing for themselves, refining the original recipe, thus informing the original owners of the beer recipe at the Danish microbrewery of the attributes people wanted in a cool beer. Because not every beer lover wants to start his own brewing operation, the original brewery also gained an entire beer product line, since accepting this user feedback into the original beer recipe also greatly increased beer sales. Just knowing that they had an impact on the revised recipe motivated the beer trendsetters, the Freebeer CLN, to buy plenty of freshly brewed Freebeer.

Giant Swiss retailer Migros provides another great example of how to leverage a CLN. When Migros created a new low-cost product line called M-Budget, it relied heavily on a large-scale CLN to choose what products to put into the line. The basic idea of M-Budget is to cannibalize some of the retailer's most successful products by selling them in generic green packaging at a much lower price. This means that M-Budget products are pretty high quality, with the lower price coming from unified packaging and branding. For example, some of Migros's best-selling cookies that were previously sold in fancy boxes are now sold at a reduced price as M-Budget cookies in the simple

FIGURE 5-1. Migros M-Budget product line.

green packaging. In 2008, M-Budget included about 500 products, ranging from food items (e.g., butter, cookies, cheese, and yogurts) to mobile phones to budget cars (through the participation of a car-sharing company in the program).

The big question Migros essentially wants to answer is: What are the attributes of cool? In other words, which existing products should be rebranded as M-Budget, thus reducing the profit margin while, hopefully, more than making up for it by increasing market share? To answer this question, Migros goes to its swarm. It organizes dozens of M-Budget parties, sponsoring rock concerts and sports events such as skateboarding competitions. At these parties it gives away M-Budget products for free. There, the young and hip are acting as free trendsetters, telling Migros what products they want under the M-Budget label (Figure 5-1). The swarm told Migros they wanted M-Budget mobile phones, M-Budget car sharing, even bathing suits in the M-Budget design. So far M-Budget sales growth has been nothing but stellar. According to the Swiss annual brand-name rankings, M-Budget has become one of the most valuable brands in Switzerland in just a few years.

CLNs don't have to be oriented toward the outside, or even involve clients at all. BlueShirt Nation is an effort by U.S. giant electronics retailer Best Buy to create an internal social networking site, where 20,000 employees have a profile page and exchange information about everything from pets to company concerns. BlueShirt Nation takes its name from the blue T-shirts that Best Buy's employees wear at work. It was created by two enterprising mid-level IT managers, on a shoestring budget, using open-source technologies. It has already proved its worth in many different aspects. It helped increase acceptance of the 401(k) plan, its users are much less likely to leave the company, and it has also been a testing ground and gathering place for new innovative ideas and products. This is a prime example of a CLN for internal use.

Listening to the swarm is not just a recipe for success in retail, but it also can help the sales force. Japanese printer and copier company Fuji Xerox Co., Ltd. (called simply Fuji Xerox henceforth) has been leveraging a Collaborative Learning Network to train its salespeople to sell an entirely new service outside its existing product and services lines.

Increasing Sales Through a CLN of Salespeople

When Japanese high-tech company Fuji Xerox decided to revamp its product and services line, it also chose new ways to educate, train, and connect its sales force. For decades Fuji Xerox had been providing office products such as copying machines and printers in Japan and abroad. But the advent of the broadband society demanded radical change from Fuji Xerox. In a shift from its longtime strategy, the company introduced a very different product, a networking service called "beat." It is a box (an inexpensive appliance server) for secure networking that is very easy to install and maintain for small and medium-size companies. After initial installation, the software features of "beat" basically take over and provide the network security services such as intrusion detection and firewall protection.

Getting people to rent a box for a few hundred dollars per month requires different sales skills. Fuji Xerox's sales force was used to selling contracts worth thousands of dollars for large copiers and printers, which are expensive to buy and expensive to maintain. The existing sales infrastructure consisted of a distributed network of sales subsidiaries. The teams of salespeople in those subsidiaries were used to dealing with procurement officers at large corporations, not renting small, cheap networking boxes to the IT department. To support the sales force in selling this new service, which went against their conventional way of selling, Fuji Xerox relied on various electronic means of communication. Even before the product was officially launched, the "beat" service department established a mailing list for communication with the salespeople as one of the main means of sharing new product information, sales tips, and service problems. Since the "beat" service was officially launched, the service department also added call centers, dedicated sales conferences, and internal newsletters for communication with the sales force.

Some of my colleagues at the MIT Center for Collective Intelligence closely monitored how the Fuji Xerox sales force changed its behavior from a hierarchically operating and communicating organization to one collaborating in COINs and Collaborative Learning Networks.[1] In particular, they monitored the mailing list used by the sales reps to communicate. They also interviewed some of the salespeople and some members of the service department.

The first thing my colleagues noticed was that the service department, although much smaller in size, posted on average about ten times more messages to the mailing list per staff member than the salespeople themselves. It turned out that salespeople and the members of the service department had formed a CLN, with the service department forming the core COIN, giving new product information and advice to the less active, and therefore more peripheral, salespeople, who formed the outer part of the learning network. This was true in the geographical sense also, with the fifty or so members of the service department being located at one office, and the roughly 15,000 salespeople being spread out over multiple sales subsidiaries.

Thorough analysis of the mailing list yielded some interesting findings. First of all, my colleagues noticed two clearly distinguishable phases. For the first two years, there was mostly communication between the service department and the salespeople, with very little communication taking place among the salespeople. This changed dramatically for the next two years, when the salespeople began using the mailing list to exchange information among themselves. This means that the CLN members had soaked up enough technical knowledge from their instructors, the members of the service department, and were now in a position to exchange sales tricks and service tips among themselves. For example, one salesman was asked by his customer about compatibility of the network box with mobile phone service. When the salesman posted this question on the mailing list, it was positively answered by another salesman, who had resolved the same question for his own customer one year earlier.

As a side benefit, the learning network also fed back new insights to the COIN, such as when salespeople discovered fixes to service glitches that the members of the service department were not aware of.

The members of the COIN of service developers were great coolfarmers. They started using the mailing list as a filter mechanism for learning about new customer needs. They picked the most demanding users, who they then would call and ask for an opportunity to visit with. A personal visit with the customer permitted them to learn first-hand about customer needs and to develop new features in collaboration with these demanding customers. They also tried to learn as much as they could from the experience of the salespeople. In the beginning the developers of the network box were the main evangelists, actively spreading the word about their new service and providing hands-on support to the salespeople in writing offers and solving the technical problems of their potential customers. Sometimes they even went with them on sales calls to potential customers. This way trust was rapidly built up between service developers—the COIN—and salespeople—the CLN.

> **COOLFARMING LESSON: The CLN will teach the COIN.**
> Once the service hit the market and salespeople started gaining experience selling and supporting the network box, the developers went out of their way to integrate this feedback into new versions of the "beat" product. Over the course of the lifetime of the service, the mode of communication between COIN and CLN changed. Initially service developers interacted in a hub-and-spoke model with salespeople face-to-face and one-on-one. Later, with the growing success of the service, they increased their two service conferences per year to four, and they also set up two different call centers to answer sales and technical questions. But more important, the communication mode changed to a peer-to-peer model among the salespeople, who asked and gave advice to each other.

Members of the sales force even started to create their own COINs. For example, one salesman asked if he could combine the network box with a so-called "mission-critical" computer server from a computer company. Other technically savvy salespeople joined him, and together they developed a new service offering that combined their own network "beat" box with the server, supported by some service developers from the original core COIN. There were also smaller COINs developing, where salespeople got together in self-organizing groups to collect structured information about competitors and their services. In other COINs, the salespeople shared and developed novel go-to-market strategies for selling the network box.

The activity on the mailing list also predicted the number of sales. The more active and excited the salespeople became, the more they started selling the network boxes. The conclusion seems obvious: The more you get your salespeople into a dialogue with the service developers, the more they will learn about the service, and the better they will be able to sell it later on. Fuji Xerox reaped huge rewards by turning its network of sales subsidiaries into a Collaborative Learning Network.

Learning About Innovations Through the P&G Technology Entrepreneurs

CLNs are also a highly efficient means of discovering new business opportunities and new products. Procter & Gamble Company has set up a successful Collaborative Learning Network of coolhunters and coolfarmers. Officially dubbed "Technology Entrepreneurs," about 90 P&G employees—mostly senior staff members from different business units and different regions of the world—were given the task of looking out for new product ideas. Started by P&G Vice President of Innovation Larry Huston, the Connect + Develop initiative has brought spectacular growth in revenue and profits to P&G.

The goal of the Technology Entrepreneurs is not to hunt for internal innovation, but to spot ideas of others outside the company. Subsequently, P&G will approach the owners of these ideas. These are individuals, small companies, or even large competitors of P&G.

According to Mark Peterson, one of the successors of Larry Huston, P&G consistently gets much higher returns from the products it brings to market based on these externally coolhunted ideas than from the products it generates internally in its own research labs. This result is consistent with the findings of MIT professor and user-driven innovation guru Erich Von Hippel. Von Hippel compared returns on products invented by corporate research labs with products suggested by end-users. Looking at the new products brought to market by famously innovative company 3M, for example, he found that the returns on end-user-developed products were two to three times higher than internally developed products.

Based on this insight, P&G started looking aggressively for outside ideas shortly after 2000. With more than $83 billion in sales in 2008, P&G is under huge pressure to fill its pipeline of new blockbuster products. It currently has twenty-three product lines generating more than $1 billion in sales globally each, and is constantly on the lookout for more to add to this roster. Its internal research and development organization has more than 9,000 employees, out of which 40 percent work outside of the United States. The employees come from sixty-seven nations, and include about 1,100 researchers on the PhD level. Its patent portfolio includes more than 36,000 patents. But even this impressive engine of innovation is not enough to feed P&G's hunger for new products. To sustain its current growth, P&G needs to find new product ideas that can generate $98 million every week. While its organic growth runs at from 4 percent to 6 percent, P&G would like to double that number.

To achieve these ambitious goals, P&G relies on the Technology Entrepreneurs. This Collaborative Learning Network acts as an intelligent search engine. P&G has a formalized search process for new products, where its business units define areas of growth and then identify potential partners, which are then systematically approached. P&G's highly skilled dealmakers subsequently negotiate the structure of the deal with the potential business partners. The best products, and the highest returns, however, come from unexpected products and opportunities. P&G is continuously looking for new disruptive technologies, for new business models, for improved ways to reach customers, and for participation in new channels. Toward that goal, it scans its own licensees, its competitors, and its suppliers. But it casts a much wider net by also scouring the output of research institutions, venture capitalists, the P&G alumni network, and design houses. And then, of course, it sends out the Technology Entrepreneurs.

The Technology Entrepreneurs are experienced R&D managers who are globally dispersed in the United States, Europe, China, Japan, Latin America, and India. They are embedded in the business units and make the initial connection to new external technologies. They focus on more strategic and bigger needs that ideally are close to market readiness. Their job is to extend P&G's capability and dialogue with external sources to find new leads and connection opportunities. This way, P&G has built a fast and efficient vetting system for new leads, vastly improving its ability to develop effective external partnerships and new business models. P&G's success with this initiative has been overwhelming. And the best part is that it is a game of give-and-take: While 42 percent of P&G's products now have a major component that comes from outside the company, P&G's internally developed ideas also generate more than $3 billion in revenue for business partners of P&G. In 2008 alone, P&G reported over a thousand new product ideas coming from the Technology Entrepreneurs.

For example, P&G's partnership with small French research company Sederma led to a highly successful skin cream. Sederma presented data at a technical conference where it showed that its new chemical compound was highly efficient in wrinkle reduction of the human skin. One of P&G's Technology Entrepreneurs sat in on this presentation, followed up on the idea, and secured the exclusive rights for Sederma's new compound for P&G. The resulting product, launched as Olay Regenerist, became a resounding success and top contributor to Olay's double-digit growth. Today, P&G is collaborating with Sederma on new anti-aging products in a win-win relationship.

In another success story, a P&G Technology Entrepreneur in Japan spotted a cleaning product in Japanese supermarkets he had never seen outside of Japan. Japanese company Unicharm had developed a duster made of fibers that are much better at collecting dust—in fact, they almost attract dust. Within eighteen months, P&G acquired the rights to the duster outside of Japan and launched it under the brand name Swiffer Duster, generating substantial revenue in almost all markets outside of Japan. P&G was even able to reuse Unicharm's advertising for its global marketing campaign.

Sometimes P&G's Technology Entrepreneurs also discover cool products from direct competitors. For example, P&G established a highly successful collaboration with competitor and leading detergent maker Clorox Company. To develop new products jointly, P&G contributed its production technology while Clorox provided the basic product, the distribution and marketing processes, and the brand name. In this case P&G basically got a finished product from a well-established competitor and used its well-oiled marketing machinery to push it globally. This level of collaboration would have been impossible just a few years ago. Today, according to both partners, this joint venture has been a huge success. According to P&G's director of external business development, Mark Peterson, P&G estimates that it generated five times more profits through the joint venture than if it had tried to develop and market the same products globally on its own. But Clorox also profited handsomely. Thanks to

P&G's marketing clout, it was able to increase market share for the jointly developed and marketed products by 5 percent to 14 percent, a huge increase in a widely saturated market where new customer needs have to be created first.

P&G collaborated with two companies at the same time to introduce a new line of candles. To develop Febreze Candles, P&G teamed up with a major candle company and Changing Paradigm, a marketing, sales, and manufacturing company in Ohio. P&G succeeded in getting a new product to market that grew by 40 percent after the launch and achieved the leadership share in its category five weeks after the launch, with a 31 percent market share.

In another partnership, P&G collaborated in selling packaged coffee beans in Dunkin' Donuts stores and elsewhere. Dunkin' Donuts is providing its trademark and formula, opening up new retail opportunities for P&G to sell packaged coffee. Again, the value proposition for both partners in this deal is compelling. Dunkin' Donuts can build on its brand equity, leverage its strength in the Northeast to expand westward with the help of P&G, and grow a "store in store" business. P&G, on the other hand, can now compete in the gourmet food segment without having to enter the restaurant business, instead generating sales by leveraging the strong Dunkin' Donuts brand.

COOLFARMING LESSON: Advertise your success to attract more success.

The most amazing thing is that P&G is not keeping its collaboration success as a well-guarded secret, but rather is talking about it widely. P&G managers like Mark Peterson are doing a very active waggle dance, advertising the two-way benefits of collaboration to potential suitors. The principle is "do good things, and tell others about it." Hopefully others will then come forward, contacting P&G's Technology Entrepreneurs. P&G even has set up a web portal, pgconnectdevelop.com, which it widely advertises. As an active coolfarmer, P&G lists its expertise for hire as well as its needs, inviting others to submit proposals for collaboration.

P&G has been quite successful in leveraging a CLN to both cool-hunt for new products and then coolfarm them jointly with other CLN members outside P&G's company boundary. But CLNs also find applications outside of the conventional business world. For example, a successful author of vampire novels uses a CLN to shape the plots of the stories jointly with her readers.

Coolfarming in *Twilight*

Author Stephenie Meyer has taken online interaction with her readers to the next level.[2] Her *Twilight* book series is about Edward Cullen, a good-looking young vampire who is in love with Bella Swan, an ordinary girl. The *Twilight* series has attracted a multimillion-reader audience in just a few years. When her fourth novel, *Breaking Dawn*, came out, she sold 3.7 million copies within the first four days. Her phenomenal success raises comparisons with the Harry Potter books. Obviously, her stories about the tangled relationship between the vampire and the girl hit a chord with readers right from the beginning. When her first book came out in 2005, she landed a contract for $750,000 for the first three books, a vast amount of money for a new and unknown author. Her rapidly increasing readership quickly confirmed the judgment of the publisher, and has been exponentially growing ever since.

Stephenie Meyer's success is not just due to her vivid imagination and superb writing skills, but also to the way she coolfarms her online community of loyal readers. From the beginning, she engaged in an online dialogue with her most loyal fans. When the first book came out, her publisher set up a standard website. Then Stephenie decided that she wanted another website more suitable to her own personality, so she set up one for herself. This site, stephe-niemeyer.com, mirrors her bubbly and friendly personality. In the early days of her success she was extremely approachable, personally answering the many questions about the intertwined fate of her heroes Edward Cullen and Bella Swan. Meyer's website is also extremely personal, revealing a lot about herself and her feelings while she conceived and continuously develops the *Twilight* series.

Although the main storyline of *Twilight* comes from the realm of fantasy, teenage readers connect extremely well to the angst and emotional turmoil of the heroes. Very quickly, dedicated readers set up online forums and blogs to connect and exchange their own sim-ilar experiences. There is even Twilight Saga, a user-maintained com-munity using a wiki, a website editable by end-users. On the Twilight Saga wiki, loyal readers have set up a biographical lexicon of the cast of the *Twilight* novels. On the social networking site MySpace, there are different *Twilight* series groups with thousands of members each, some of them set up soon after the first *Twilight* novel appeared.

When Stephenie Meyer discovered these groups on MySpace, she quickly joined and answered the questions of the fans. After reader Lori Joffs posted the *Twilight* story viewed from the side of Edward the vampire instead of Bella the girl, Stephenie posted a flattering review on her website, saying "I'm having a great time reading your vision of things." Encouraged by Stephenie's support, Lori Joffs contacted the author and offered to create Twilight Lexicon, a fan website collecting all the facts about the series. Stephenie enthusiastically embraced the idea and gladly provided bios of the major characters of her novels, as well as a timeline of the story. This is coolfarming at its best; an early and committed COIN member, Lori, offering her wholehearted support—for free and for the cause—to get the idea off the ground. The creator—Stephenie—chimes in, and in turn supports the first COIN members spiritually and emotionally, but not financially. According to *BusinessWeek*,[3] Twilight Lexicon is now the most active *Twilight* website, with 30,000 daily visitors.

Using her own website, Stephenie Meyer engages in intensive face-to-face contact with her readers. She has arranged "I love Edward" parties in libraries and bookstores, where large numbers of her readers showed up. When Kady Weatherford, one of her readers, joked that she should throw a *Twilight* prom, Stephenie jumped on the suggestion. Her publisher also was very supportive of the idea. The 500-person event sold out in six hours once it was advertised on her website. Additional proms also sold out very quickly, and when Meyer launched *Eclipse*, her next book, in 2007, thousands of people came to her book signings.

Besides her original audience, teenage readers, a second fan base of peers popped up. TwilightMOMS is the community of mothers of *Twilight*-reading teenagers, many of them avid readers of the *Twilight* stories themselves. Again, Stephenie showed her mastery of coolfarming by posting on the TwilightMOMS website: "Hi, my fellow moms, it's just so cool that I'm not the only 30+ mom and wife in love with fictional underage vampires and werewolves."

In the meantime, TwilightMOMS is bustling with life, and moms on the forums are discussing all aspects of *Twilight*-influenced family life.

COOLFARMING LESSON: Be nice to the members of your CLN.
Besides the MySpace pages, the Twilight Saga wiki, the Twilight Lexicon, and TwilightMOMS, Stephenie lists over 300 fan websites of her books on her own site. The online discussion forums provide a first-rate Collaborative Learning Network for

her to read the pulse and taste of her readers. Stephenie Meyer is a successful creator and coolfarmer. She is very approachable (well, as reachable as still possible with millions of demanding fans) and personable. She is genuine in personal contact and comes across not as an elite author, but as "one of us."

Six Guidelines for CLNs

1. Let the CLN teach the COIN. At first, the salespeople at Fuji Xerox (the CLN) learned about their new product from the service developers (the core COIN). But after two years, the salespeople had enough technical knowledge and firsthand experience so that they could communicate important information to each other. In addition, the CLN fed back new insights to the COIN, as salespeople discovered solutions to problems that the service department had not yet encountered.

2. Advertise your success to find more success. Procter & Gamble does not keep its multiple collaborations secret. Instead, P&G makes sure to spread the word about its successful collaborations. P&G managers are doing a very active "waggle dance," advertising the two-way benefits to potential suitors, encouraging them to come forward with their own proposals.

3. Be nice to the members of your CLN. Best-selling author Stephenie Meyer has stayed in touch with her readers by engaging in an online dialogue with her most loyal fans. She personally answers questions about the *Twilight* books, as well as supports and encourages her fans in their own *Twilight*-related projects. She is also humble enough to take her readers' input to shape her plot.

4. Learn about your product from your market. CLNs are a magnificent way to learn about the needs of your market and to get feedback from real users for new features. Fuji Xerox's service developers reached out to the company's salespeople, making them part of the extended service development and testing system team. As a result, the service developers were able to learn about customer needs and develop new features in collaboration with the most demanding customers.

5. Find the attributes of cool. Listening to the CLN will tell the creators what the user community thinks are the cool things they appreciate most about the new product. Swiss retail giant Migros created a highly successful budget product line by asking consumers—especially hip, young trendsetters—which of Migros's products they wanted to see available at lower prices. The swarm helped the company choose the coolest products for repackaging and branding.

6. Find the locations for the hive. The CLN is a useful coolhunting network, with the CLN members coming back to the COIN and telling it in what direction to go. Just like the P&G Technology Entrepreneurs, who spot highly profitable business opportunities for P&G outside of the core P&G ecosystem, CLN members are great coolhunters. Respect the members of the CLN, because they will be the greatest supporters of the COIN and important teachers of what works and what does not!

Once the COIN has honed the product to the tastes of the CLN, time has come to launch an all-out viral marketing campaign, to get the new trendy product over the tipping point. And that's where the CIN—the Collaborative Interest Network—comes in.

6

CIN
Building the Buzz

Vox populi, vox dei: "The voice of people is the voice of God!"

IN THE FINAL phase of coolfarming, the Collaborative Innovation Network and the Collaborative Learning Network band together to spread the word. Together, they get the world to embrace the new product and spend actual money to buy it. Humans are no different from the bee coolhunters, who beep at their sisters in the swarm until the heat of the swarm gets over a threshold and the bee swarm explodes and flies off in a new direction. In precisely the same way, the human swarm must take off and follow the trendsetters. Through word-of-mouth marketing, a Collaborative Interest

Network (CIN) will emerge naturally and spread the word. This community of people, who think the new product is incredibly cool, will build unstoppable momentum, making the product a resounding success.

Through viral marketing, members of the COIN and CLN find the outsiders who are the influencers and convince others to jump on the bandwagon. This process is what carries the idea or new product over the tipping point and makes it a real trend in the outside world. The CLN members are masters of the art of finding the role models who are not just accepted but highly admired by the target group. Once those role models are found, they should not be bought—rather, they must be convinced by the merits of the idea. Ideally, this idea is a worthy cause that the role models care about deeply, causing them to invest their entire reputation and energy to get it off the ground.

Just one admired role model can change the behavior of many people. Consider, for example, how Oprah's Book Club generated renewed interest in Leo Tolstoy's *Anna Karenina*, a literary classic that many Americans otherwise might not have experienced.

Another excellent example is the way Migros markets its low-budget M-Budget products, as introduced in the previous chapter. To better understand the needs of its customer base, Migros organizes M-Budget parties, where cool kids can try products for free. Migros also sponsors contemporary music bands to further increase participation at the parties. As a result, buyers of M-Budget products aren't stigmatized for not being able to afford more expensive, high-end food and consumer products, but are instead associated with the cool kids at the M-Budget parties, and are thus considered cool also. These kids at the parties form not just a CLN, but also an important Collaborative Interest Network, building up the heat in the swarm and "beeping at" the other potential customers.

Apple's Steve Jobs is a master of building up the heat, raising the buzz until his dedicated swarm of loyal Apple users can't wait anymore to get their hands on the next iPhone, iPod, or MacBook. Once the new product is launched with much fanfare, Jobs makes sure to introduce artificial scarcity, by not having enough of the product initially. When the new iPhone came out in spring 2008, the lines at the Apple store in Cambridge went around the block twice. Customers waited patiently in line for many hours, until they finally could lay their hand on one of the prized iPhones. The heat of the swarm was close to boiling.

For yet another example of how to create cool trends through viral marketing in CLNs and CINs, let's look at the way LEGO develops and markets its robot Mindstorms toy toolkit.

Immersion Gets the Swarm to Explosion— LEGO Mindstorms

Over the last decade, privately held Danish toy brick producer LEGO has become a master coolfarmer. Long renowned for the way it harnessed creative ideas, LEGO has completely revamped how it develops new products. Many innovative people attribute their attitude and the way in which they develop new products to their childhood experience playing with LEGO bricks. LEGO is one of the strongest brands in the toy world, commanding premium prices from a fiercely loyal following around the globe. Still majority-owned by the founding family, LEGO started in 1932 as a producer of wooden toys. In the sixties, the first version of the familiar plastic bricks was added to the product list, and since then LEGO has continuously innovated by coming up with new ways of using the bricks to foster the creativity, imagination, and invention of children, who frequently remain loyal users of the toy bricks even as adults.

LEGO bricks have been used to build life-size models of dinosaurs, prototype biometric retina scanners, and artificial robotic hands. Since the invention of the original plastic brick, LEGO has come a long way by tapping into the creativity of its users. Originally, LEGO hired some of the most enthusiastic users of its toys as developers of new versions and models of LEGO toys. It later teamed up with users, inviting them to contribute ideas for new LEGO brick models that might be turned into new products. Initially, these new products were then marketed by LEGO. Today, this approach is being taken to the next step, and users themselves are invited to independently develop, market, and sell their LEGO brick-based products on eBay and through conventional sales channels. This LEGO-based ecosystem has reached a level of maturity where user-started companies collaborate with LEGO on even terms, coming up with new uses of LEGO bricks never dreamed up by LEGO itself.

LEGO Mindstorms is a particularly good example. Mindstorms is a set of programmable LEGO bricks that combines a full-fledged programming environment with electric motors, sensors, LEGO Technic pieces, and bricks. The first versions of LEGO Mindstorms were developed jointly with the MIT Media Lab. Since their inception in 1998 they have been bought by about 80,000 people per year throughout the world, basically without any marketing at all. About one million kits are currently on the market. Just doing a video search on YouTube brings up more than 3,800 videos where users display novel uses of Mindstorms.

Within weeks of the original Mindstorms launch, a graduate student from Stanford University had hacked the interface between the PC and the Mindstorms robot and published it on the Web. Quickly, other Mindstorms fans used his findings to develop a new programming language and operating system, replacing the one provided by LEGO. When LEGO discovered that its proprietary code was freely accessible on the Internet, its first instinct was to set loose its powerful legal team to rein in the Mindstorms hackers. But a few weeks of observation convinced LEGO that a much better approach would be to leverage the creativity and inspirational ideas of the Mindstorms hackers for its own use. Instead of writing "cease-and-desist letters," LEGO wrote a "right to hack" into the Mindstorms software license. Soon, a bustling universe of Mindstorms extensions and applications surfaced, ranging from robot-controlled LEGO car factories to bowling robots and solvers of Rubik's Cube, to toilet-paper folders, soda machines, and bubble gum sorters. Hardware gurus created new high-quality sensors for uses LEGO never had thought of.

In 2005, when LEGO decided to develop the next version of Mindstorms, it turned to coolhunting and coolfarming. First, it looked for the most loyal and most innovative users. Coolhunting through online forums, mailing lists, and blogs of LEGO Mindstorms addicts, LEGO tried to find the Mindstorms users who were considered the most respected, influential, and creative by their peers. LEGO's cool-hunt resulted in a list of twenty names. Further winnowing brought the list down to four names: Steve Hassenplug, John Barnes, David Schilling, and Ralph Hempel.

When approached by LEGO, the four agreed to sign a nondisclosure agreement. They already knew each other from Brickfest, the annual gathering of LEGO addicts, where the zealots show each other their most elegant and daring creations. They were then brought into a secure online forum, where they could touch base electronically and speculate about their task. Initially left in the dark, they wondered if they might be invited to be early testers of the next version of Mindstorms. After about two weeks, Søren Lund, the director of Mindstorms, joined their discussion on the forum. The four were quite surprised when Lund told them that LEGO was still far away from having a finished version of the next Mindstorms version. Lund then explained LEGO's idea of the process of how to create the next version of Mindstorms. To develop the new product, LEGO wanted to collaborate much closer with its lead users, in a way it had never done it before. The goal was to create a MUP, a LEGO Mindstorms user panel. When the four agreed to be the first MUP, they formed an initial COIN, collaborating closely with LEGO on the development of the new version of Mindstorms.

Sworn to absolute secrecy by LEGO, over the next eleven months they became de facto members of the core LEGO team of Mindstorms creators. LEGO wanted to keep the next version of Mindstorms entirely out of the public spotlight, both because competitors were eager to learn about LEGO's plans and also to be able to launch the new version with a big bang. The COIN exchanged countless e-mails with Lund and his team, meeting him at the annual Brickfest and even flying to LEGO's headquarters to discuss some new features. One key fact about the four COIN members—they were not paid any money at all. They even paid their own airfare to fly to Denmark. They were only given some LEGO crane sets and proto-types of the new version of Mindstorms. The four unanimously agreed: "They're going to talk to us about Legos, and they're going to pay us with Legos! They actually want our opinion? It doesn't get much better than that."[1]

LEGO drew heavily on the expertise of its initial COIN members. Ralph Hempel, highly respected for creating pbForth, another version of the Mindstorms software, helped with the development of the new robot programming toolkit. John Barnes was famed for creating a new type of ultrasonic sensor. When LEGO asked him if he would mind if they integrated his sensors into the new version of Mindstorms, he told them to just go ahead and do it. In another example, the COIN discovered that it was difficult to make rectangular designs with the new type of bricks LEGO intended to use in the next version of Mindstorms. At their suggestion, LEGO added a special part to the original kit to address this problem.

The new version of Mindstorms was a radical innovation compared to its two predecessor versions. It could not be used with older versions of Mindstorms. It used not only the basic LEGO bricks as building blocks, but also their much sleeker cousins from the LEGO Technic series. Søren Lund, the main developer, wanted to create a much easier-to-use version. One of the main obstacles of the previous versions had been their complexity. This complexity was one of the main reasons that half of all Mindstorms users were not children—the intended audience—but tinkering adults such as Hassenplug, Barnes, Schilling, and Hempel. LEGO also teamed up with an external software development company to come up with an easier-to-use programming environment, some sort of Photoshop for robotics. When members of LEGO's executive board were invited to be alpha-testers of the new program, it took them just twenty minutes to create their first robot.

To decide on the new features, besides its core COIN of four creators, LEGO also drew on the online forums of Mindstorms users. It relied on the full ecosystem of COINs, CLNs, and CINs. For example, the biggest complaint in the online user forums was the reliance on a fickle infrared connection to transmit instructions from the PC to the Mindstorms robot. Therefore, Lund and his team decided to replace infrared with a USB connection.

The COIN did not meet face-to-face with Lund until after the Brickfest conference, where they got together to finalize the parts that would go into the basic Mindstorms toolkit. Although playing a vital role in the development of the new version of Mindstorms, the COIN members were never paid, as mentioned previously. When Lund asked them why they were doing it, Barnes told him: "I did it because it was the LEGO company. I would not do it for another company. . . . It's an honor to be asked."[2]

After the Brickfest, LEGO extended the initial MUP COIN, growing it into a CLN, a Collaborative Learning Network. After the first ten months, another seven MUP members were brought in, joining the original four to broaden the user base and learn from a larger group of lead users and innovators. Another five months later, in March 2006, LEGO put out the word that it was looking for about 100 more MUP members. Out of the 9,600 Mindstorms developers, this third wave of another 100 lead users didn't just form a larger CLN, it became the nucleus of a Collaborative Interest Network, a CIN.

Since then, LEGO has been honing its skills at coolfarming. It is further growing its CLNs into a CIN. Its online forum NXTLOG (see Figure 6–1) contained more than 6,000 projects as of July 2008. It does a masterful job of community building, displaying featured projects, latest projects, and top-ranked projects.

User innovators can map out and plan new Mindstorms robots using LDRAW, a user-developed computer drawing tool, where building instructions, parts lists, and other instructions can be accessed for printout or further modification.

Users have been developing a wealth of new hardware. All types of sensors, such as accelerometers, compasses, and many others, are sprouting up. Users market them on eBay, with the explicit blessing, and sometimes even active support, of LEGO. For example, LEGO's line of HiTechnic products, mostly sensors for Mindstorms, is now further developed and marketed by a business partner in close collaboration with LEGO. According to LEGO, this partnership is highly beneficial and lucrative for both business partners.

On the low range of technology, LEGO has developed an entry-level version of Mindstorms for the OLPC, the $100 laptop computer originally conceived by MIT Media Lab founder Nicholas Negroponte (see Chapter 3). This version has already

FIGURE 6-1. NXTLOG Community page on the Mindstorms website. ©2009 The LEGO Group. Used here by special permission.

been successfully introduced and tested in Brazil, one of the early users of the OLPC.

In a sense, LEGO's openness toward the Mindstorms hackers was a natural extension of its approach of encouraging the creativity of its users. LEGO has set up an Internet-based fan club with do-it-yourself kits and blueprints. It has even created the LEGO factory, a customization program that lets LEGO users design, upload, and purchase their own customized LEGO creation. Using the LEGO Digital Designer software, users can design a LEGO model whose bricks will afterward be packaged and shipped to the original designer. Users can show off their designs in an online gallery to share them with the rest of the world. Afterward, they can order the bricks needed to build their model, even designing their own package box. LEGO is tapping into this collective intelligence for inspiration and to come up with new product ideas for mass-market models. For example, in March 2006, ten lead users designed seventy-six different train models, out of which a series of LEGO-designed products was brought to the market.

LEGO also took this community-based approach to educational innovation to regional markets. Under the name LEGO Zoom, a program in Brazil connects close to a thousand public schools, sending students to face-to-face meetings but also connecting them through an online community and website. The goal is to come up with new and innovative uses of LEGO bricks to study and teach math, science, and other subjects from the elementary to the middle-school level. A set of LEGO kits now teaches in a "learning by doing" approach all aspects of energy, energy conservation, and physics.

LEGO Brickstructures is the poster child of a new collaboration model between small inventors and LEGO. When Adam Tucker, an architect in Chicago, came up with the idea to market models of famous landmark buildings such as the Sears Tower in his hometown, LEGO decided not to usurp his idea but to partner with the tiny start-up and jointly mass-market a first batch of 1,250 sets.

No project is too wild not to be tackled by COINs of hardcore LEGO fans. Currently, there is heated discussion on LEGO Mindstorms forums about what it would take to land a LEGO Moonbot on the moon in order to win the $30 million Google Lunar X Prize. The goal of the Lunar X Prize challenge is to get a privately funded spacecraft on the moon, landing a robot that will have to successfully roam the lunar surface for at least 500 meters and then send back a data packet to Earth. The discussion on the forum nicely laid out the problems, while already providing possible solutions to most of them—nothing seems impossible or out of reach for a dedicated

COIN! In 2008, the project was officially launched, supported by LEGO, BBC, NASA, and other heavyweight players. They hope to test a first version on Earth by 2010, and to have a first mission launch by 2013 to 2016.

COOLFARMING LESSON: Delegate power to the swarm.
Similar to Apple, LEGO has succeeded in creating and inspiring brand loyalty through a CLN/CIN-based ecosystem that is far beyond the usual. But while Apple's appeal is mostly thanks to one man's genius in reading the collective mind of his products' target customers, LEGO's success is due to a committed and immensely loyal swarm of fans and creative innovators, a Collaborative Interest Network if there ever was one. LEGO tattoos and LEGO vanity license plates are just some small indicators at the tip of the iceberg of an immensely committed community.

Building the Heat—Yummy Industries

You don't need the resources of a multibillion-dollar company like LEGO for successful coolfarming through a Collaborative Interest Network. Two artists and designers, Francesca and Bernhard, prove otherwise.

Bernhard and Francesca (known only by their first names) met some ten years ago in the Art and Design University in Los Angeles. Ever since, they have been a team, both privately and professionally. He is the Swiss conceptual thinker, she the visual designer of Italian and English descent. While they have been coolhunting new ideas for their entire lives, when they returned from LA to Basel, Switzerland, they started coolfarming in earnest. There was never a shortage of ideas; rather, there were so many that they have had a hard time prioritizing. As Bernhard explained to me, "It is not about making money, but about the idea, and about combining the real and the virtual world."

One of their first projects when they came back from the United States was working as artists for the clothing design fair Bread & Butter, itself a compelling example of coolfarming. Bread & Butter was launched by three Germans: Kristyan Geyr, Wolfgang Ahlers, and Karl-Heinz Müller. In 2000, they decided that they wanted to start an alternative clothing design fair in an old factory in Cologne. The fair would not just be a showcase for designer clothes but a far-more-entertaining half arts show, half party. From day one, the fair was a smashing success. Their recipe—mix artists like Bernard and Francesca with owners of fashion labels who were peddling their wares to boutique owners and buyers from large retailers—proved irresistible.

The Noodles, as the three Germans called themselves, were able to draw on a vast network of artists to spruce up their fair. They turned the selling and buying of fashion into a three-day party that quickly became the ultimate in cool. After two years, Cologne became too small, and the Noodles moved Bread & Butter to Berlin, where it quickly grew to over a thousand vendors and a hundred thousand visitors. After another two years, Berlin became too small again. Bread & Butter is now held in Barcelona, where it established itself as a major annual artistic and commercial event.

COOLFARMING LESSON: Organize loosely, knit tightly!
The Noodles proved their coolfarming talent, drawing on a loosely organized but tightly knit group of some twenty artists, designers, lighting professionals, and organizers to reach the Collaborative Interest Network of thousands of bulk buyers of fashion. Their swarm ranges from owners of small

FIGURE 6–2. Yummy key tie.

clothing and fashion shops to the fashion procurement officers of large retail chains such as Target and upmarket clothing store chains such as Gap, Abercrombie & Fitch, and Liz
Claiborne. By turning their event into the pinnacle of cool,
they have been able to convince the swarm.

***COOLFARMING LESSON: Idea comes first, making money
follows later.***

Bernhard and Francesca, meanwhile, finally got their breakthrough with their key ties (see Figure 6–2). In response to the
demands of "having to wear a tie," they are inviting the fash-
ionable gentleman to wear his tie in his pant pocket, using the
tie like a key ring. Their key tie became quite successful; so
much so that they bought up boxes of old ties from secondhand stores as raw material for their key ties.

FIGURE 6–3. Yummy artistic belt.

The real breakthrough, however, came with their artistic belt. While their business, Yummy Industries, produces many different products besides belts and key ties—living proof of their never-ending creativity—the belts are the real money makers. The idea was born when they saw a label-weaving machine in Turkey. They were visiting a Turkish friend they had met at the design academy in Los Angeles, and he showed them a machine to weave clothing labels. This machine would not just print the washing and ironing instructions on a label, but it would weave the signs into the fabric. It struck them that the same technology could also be used to weave entire pictures on a belt. And that's what they did. Bernhard himself made the first belt designs (see Figure 6–3).

Immediately he reached out to his COIN of artistic friends. He made sure that from the beginning there was something in it for everybody involved. He came up with a scheme where from the first batch run of 200 artistic belts, each artist friend would get thirty-three to sell. This forced the individual artist to also become a microentrepreneur. If the belt became more successful and new "print" runs were needed, Yummy Industries would now sell all the belts and pay a royalty to the artist. To design, produce, and market the belts, the Yummies (as Bernhard and Francesca are known) relentlessly tapped their Collaborative Innovation Network. They invited designer friends from the art school, but also other friends they had met at Bread & Butter and elsewhere to design new belts. They worked through their Turkish friend with the producer in Turkey who owned the weaving machine to tweak the machine for wild and crazy new designs.

Bernhard and Francesca also tapped their network of artists and friends in Basel to finish and package the belts. The Turkish entrepreneur gives them the raw belts, but to do the final production and packaging they rely on their COIN and CLN. Jointly, they produce belt racks, which they send together with their belts to the clothing stores and boutiques. They also do a brisk business selling direct from their website. Over the last three years, since they started producing the belts, their sales numbers have been growing exponentially, turning them from starving artists to these rare beasts—commercially successful artists.

The main reason for their success, however, is Bernard and Francesca's immersion into the Collaborative Interest Network. They would not have been successful in selling their belts had they not gotten the free and encompassing support of the Noodles, the Bread & Butter founders whom they had helped in the past. Not only did the Noodles offer them prime exposition space for their belts at the Bread & Butter trade show, but they also gave them high exposure through preferred coverage in their printed Bread & Butter fashion catalog and website. This way, Bernard and Francesca could build up the heat by "beeping at" their customers, the small clothing boutique owners who buy their belts and key ties and put them up for sale in their fashion stores. Supporting their face-to-face interaction with an online storefront and community further allowed them to get direct access to their end customers, collecting their feedback and gauging their response to new belt designs.

From Creators to CINs—Illustrating the Process Through Social Networks

CINs not only carry consumer products over the tipping point, but they can also help spread ideas inside large companies. In my earlier book on *Swarm Creativity*,[3] I described how collaborative innovation happens based on my own experience working in a COIN at Deloitte Consulting, where the creator-COIN-CLN-CIN process was further leveraged to develop a new consulting service focused on the Collaborative Knowledge Network (CKN).

During my time as European e-business practice leader—right when the e-business bubble was at its peak—I experienced the power of the swarm. A consultant named Robin in the Deloitte Research office in New York had the idea of bringing together a group of consultants in San Francisco, to talk about what the Internet might do for collaboration. Her plan was that we would collaboratively write what we called an "e-view," a document describing a new emergent trend about a hot topic.

Robin invited a mixed group of people. Along with my boss Cathy, the global e-business practice leader, and me, Robin also brought in her boss, the head of Deloitte Research, and some other partners and consultants she thought might work together well to develop a new point of view on this subject. The way this group of people collaborated serves as a perfect blueprint for the creator-COIN-CLN-CIN process. The process started with Robin, who was a perfect fit for the role of creator. While she was not that high up in the pecking order of Deloitte, she had built a great network of people to draw on for the creation of new ideas. And if she did not know the right people for a certain task, she certainly knew the people who knew others suited for whatever idea Robin had in mind. For example, she knew Adriaan, a senior manager for Deloitte in Texas, who was the unofficial "prophet" for knowledge management at Deloitte. Robin went to him when she was looking for creative minds to help her on her "e-view"; in fact, it was Adriaan who recommended me to Robin.

I still vividly remember the initial meeting in San Francisco, with Robin doing a perfect waggle dance for her idea. In this first meeting we laid out the blueprint for what later would become the Collaborative Knowledge Network, a concept the nascent COIN developed over the next eighteen months. Robin had selected a group of people excited about the idea of developing the "e-view." Over the next few months, some of the original members, but also a few new ones, communicated almost daily to develop the concept. As the budget was limited, after the initial meeting we mostly collaborated over the Internet. We also had biweekly web conferences that we called "virtual brown bags," where usually anywhere from a dozen to up to a hundred people got together virtually to discuss the latest thinking and new ideas on collaboration and knowledge creation.

Our communication pattern was captured very well in our e-mail exchanges, which were fully distributed to people physically located in Helsinki, Zurich, New York, San Francisco, Melbourne, and Singapore. In our online meetings, some people always had to get up in the middle of the night to participate. To retroactively better understand the communication process, I therefore loaded the e-mail archives into our Condor communication analysis tool (described in more detail in Chapter 7).

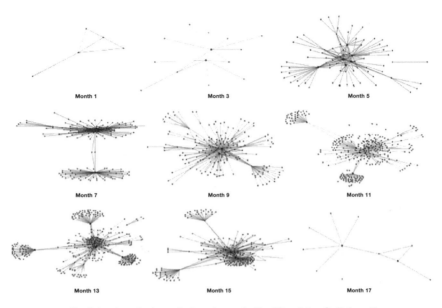

*FIGURE 6–4. Social network view of nine stages in the life of the Collaborative
Knowledge Network (CKN) community.*

Figure 6–4 illustrates the different stages in the life of this community. In the first nine months, our group focused on brainstorming and fleshing out the main ideas and the related topics suitable as
consulting services—after all, as a business, Deloitte Consulting wanted
to make productive use of the ideas we were developing. The network
pictures in Figure 6–4 were generated automatically based on the
communication in my e-mail box and the mailboxes of a few colleagues, which were loaded into the Condor social network analysis
tool. Each dot represents a person, and the connecting line means
that at least one e-mail was exchanged; the more e-mails two people
exchanged, the shorter the connecting line.

After having worked as a virtual team, we met once more face-to-
face in Robin's office in New York. It was not the same group of people anymore. Some had left the company in the meantime, but others
had joined, working to convert the vision into a real service. For
example, there was now Thomas, a colleague from the Swiss Deloitte

office, who had become another driving force within the community. Thomas had started some subgroups developing consulting services based on the general concept, while Robin was driving completion of the original e-view.

Activities from the tenth to the fifteenth month therefore shifted from idea generation to execution, where the focus was on the development of the planned new consulting products—marketing brochures, thought leadership articles, and analysis software. There were less fundamentally new ideas coming up at this time. During this second phase in the life cycle of the community, the social network pictures show a change in the social structure and a shift toward new organizational dynamics, like the decentralization of work and the emergence of dedicated subgroups for designated tasks. In other words, the COIN grew into a CLN, and later even into a CIN. For example, months nine and eleven show a typical CLN structure, with the core COIN members in the center communicating with new CLN members in the periphery. In month thirteen, the CLN expands further into a CIN, with little hubs of activity sprouting up at previously peripheral nodes representing CLN members.

Marco DiMaggio, a colleague at the University of Salento in southern Italy, further analyzed the data in the e-mail boxes, looking at what people said in their e-mail communications. This permitted Marco to filter communication by the different subprojects. Once the initial "Collaborative Knowledge Network" COIN had sprung to life, many subprojects emerged based on the personal initiative of COIN members. While Robin led the development on the original e-view, Thomas, my colleague in the Swiss office, started a "Collaborative Knowledge Network diagnostic" subproject. The COIN around Thomas developed customized software to collect and compare information about the Collaborative Knowledge Network (CKN) readiness

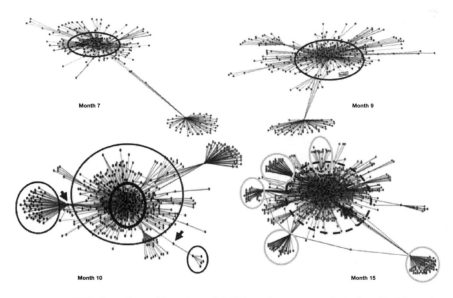

FIGURE 6–5. *Diffusion of new ideas from COIN (months seven and nine) to CLN (month ten) to CIN (month fifteen).*

of organizations. This tool was quickly adapted by consultants outside of the core COIN for marketing and revenue generation. Figure 6–5 shows the communication network of the CKN diagnostic subproject, illustrating the life cycle of a COIN focusing on a new area, from when the topic sprang to life, to its peak, to when it disappeared in a flurry of other e-mail messages.

COOLFARMING LESSON: Communication patterns show the emergence of COINs, CLNs, and CINs.

As Figure 6–5 illustrates, an emergent new COIN within the full ecosystem of CINs and CLNs can be automatically extracted by analyzing discussion content and become clearly recognizable. The "CKN diagnostics" COIN started out as a new COIN in months seven and nine in Figure 6–5, and grew to a Collaborative Learning Network by month ten, when the product was picked up by early adopters outside of the core CKN community. In month fifteen, the CLN started to grow little new clusters, a typical sign of an emergent Collaborative Interest Network. This was because the CLN members started to use the CKN diagnostics software in real-life consulting projects, while reporting back and asking for support from the original COIN around Thomas.

Five Guidelines for CINs

1. Delegate power to the swarm. Much of LEGO's success is due to an immensely devoted swarm of fans and creative innovators, an excellent example of a Collaborative Interest Network. They have tapped into their knowledge in developing new versions and models of LEGO toys, encouraging their natural creativity. In creating the new version of Mindstorms, LEGO sought out four of its most loyal and innovative users and fully involved them in the early development of the new product.

2. Organize loosely, knit tightly. Starting with the idea of an alternative clothing design fair, the Noodles created a major annual artistic and commercial event. Rather than simply holding a showcase for designer clothes, the three Germans brought together a loosely organized but close-knit group of some twenty artists, designers, lighting professionals, and organizers to reach the Collaborative Interest Network of thousands of bulk buyers of fashion.

3. Develop the idea first; making money will follow later. Bernhard and Francesca coolhunted creative new ideas for their entire lives and eventually built a profitable business, Yummy Industries, that produces a number of offbeat products, such as key ties and artistic belts. Bernard turned his many artistic friends into microentrepreneurs by letting them design new products and share in the rewards if they were successful. By relentlessly tapping their Collaborative Innovation Network of artists, the Yummies demonstrated coolfarming at its best.

4. *Build up the heat.* COIN members need to convince their swarm
of the greatness of their idea (just like the Yummies did) by beeping at
them in many different ways. Immersing themselves into the swarm
and introducing artificial scarcity, by limiting the belts to a restricted
first edition, was a method that worked for the Yummies. At Deloitte,
it was Robin, Thomas, and I who built up the heat to grow excitement
for our new consulting service based on the concept of the Collaborative Knowledge Network.

5. *Use immersive techniques to get the swarm to explode.* COINs give
away power to their most loyal users (as LEGO did), immersing
themselves into the swarm of customers. When the swarm is empow-
ered, it will be totally fired up about the new product and literally do
anything to promote and acquire it.

Once the vision of the COIN has been picked up by the
Collaborative Interest Network, it has successfully gotten over the
tipping point and is now visible to the outside world. The CIN is the
critical vehicle to convert the innovation into a real trend. The CLN
will help the COIN understand what makes the innovation cool for
the target audience, but the buzz and feedback in the CIN will make
or break the trend. There is no clear-cut boundary between CLN and
CIN, just like there is none between a CLN and COIN. Rather, people are fluctuating in and out, as we have seen repeatedly in the
LEGO, Migros, P&G, Yummy Industries, Fuji Xerox, Deloitte, and
OLPC examples. Transparency and accessibility of the creators—not
just for the COIN members, but also for other people in the CIN—
is key. Steve Jobs is still selling every new product of Apple himself.
Søren Lund, the main developer of Mindstorms, personally contacts
as many Mindstorms users as possible in LEGO's online forums. The
Fuji Xerox product developers use the CLN of salespeople to reach
out to the CIN of end-user customers.

Understanding what the people in a CIN do provides a unique opportunity to coolhunt for new product ideas for the original COIN members. And the great thing is that this way of coolhunting is not restricted to COIN members. Rather, thanks to the transparency of the Web, everybody can use this approach to discover cool trends before the rest of the world finds them. The next chapter describes a more formalized way of putting our knowledge of the creator-COIN-CLN-CIN process to productive use by hunting for cool trends in the COIN phase on the Web.

7

Coolhunting
Find the Trends Through the Trendsetters

AS WE SAW in Chapter 3, great coolfarmers are also great cool-hunters. An in-depth understanding of the coolfarming process is key for successful coolhunting, which explains why talented coolfarmers are also good in spotting new trends early on.

We are flooded every day with new ideas reaching us from all directions, through all types of media and day-to-day contact with others. But which of those ideas will become a new trend? You might think today that it is clear the iPod had to become a success, now that it has left all the other MP3 players relegated to also-ran

status. However, even products from Apple occasionally can floun-
der. I still own one of the original Newtons from Apple, the personal organizer launched in the mid-1990s, which never caught
on, while the Psion Organiser and the BlackBerry went on to dom-
inate that market for nearly a decade, until the iPhone arrived. But
there is indeed one critical success factor that distinguishes iPod
and iPhone from all its competitors, and that's the team behind the
new product.

Coolhunting means finding the cool trends before the crowd dis-
covers them. And looking at the team behind the innovative new
product is the best predictor of future success. This concept is the
foundation of our coolhunting process. The basic idea of coolhunting is very simple. Find the people who create the cool trends, and
you have also found the trends. But finding these people is not so easy.
While we have discussed the characteristics of the creator, these traits
are hard to spot from the outside. Distinguishing the next Tim
Berners-Lee from all the other innovators in the same field who will
never make it can be a huge challenge. How can we know and predict which ideas will be carried to fruition, or which tiny seeds will
grow into saplings, and then into huge trees?

If we want to find the tall trees of tomorrow, we need to look for
the seeds of today. Finding the most promising seeds in the forest
of ideas is the basic tenet of coolhunting. Each huge old tree tow-
ering over the other, smaller trees started as a tiny seed at some
point in the past (as Figure 7–1 suggests). Unfortunately, at least
from the perspective of coolhunting, there are millions and millions
of seeds. Which ones are going to grow into huge trees?

If ideas are the seeds to be grown into cool trends—the huge old
trees—then the seeds carried by intrinsically motivated people have
the best chance to succeed. The more the people nurturing and
developing the idea care about the idea instead about themselves and

FIGURE 7–1. *Coolhunting—figuring out which seeds of today will be the tall trees of tomorrow.*

their egos, the better the chances for their ideas to succeed. Those promising seeds are carried by COINs, people who are able to step over their own egos for the benefit of their ideas. If we find the most highly motivated groups assembling around an idea, and the ones generating the most buzz, we have discovered the cool trend of tomorrow! To understand in more detail how coolhunting works, let's look at how we search for a restaurant in an unfamiliar city.

Coolhunting Combines the Wisdom of Crowds, Experts, and Swarms

I once spent a few days in Paris with my children. We were the typical tourists, climbing the Eiffel Tower, visiting the Château de Versailles, and admiring *Mona Lisa* in the Louvre. We were staying in a middle-class hotel in Montmartre, a district in the north of Paris named for the hill at its center. In the evenings, we were coolhunting for good restaurants. To find value for our money, we were applying different strategies. One evening, we were just following the tourist streams. We wound up on top of Montmartre, near the cathedral of Sacré-Coeur. This is the place were all the artists are, selling their paintings and offering to draw on-the-spot portraits of tourists. It is also an area chock-full of tourist restaurants. We ended up in one of them. The food was okay—it is hard to get really bad food in Paris—

but the price was not cheap, seventy euros (about 100 US dollars), for a decent meal for three.

The next day we decided to follow the recommendation of our hotel owner and eat in his favorite restaurant. It offered excellent food at the reasonable (for a luxury restaurant) price of eighty-six euros (about 130 US dollars) for a meal for three. We were sitting beside two Germans, however, who were grumbling the entire evening because they could not get a decent beer at this restaurant. That we understood everything they were saying in German did not make it any better for us: It seems that this restaurant is recommended to many other tourists.

The third evening, we decided to follow our own instincts. We wandered around in Montmartre, peeking in at many restaurants. In the end we found one that was quite small, but also quite full, mostly with locals. It turned out to be an excellent choice. We had a great meal in the restaurant, Villa de Poulot, at a cost of forty-five euros.

What we had done in Paris was, very simply, coolhunt for the best restaurant. The first day, when we ended up in a tourist trap, we had followed the *crowd* of tourists. The next day, in the excellent but pricey restaurant, we had followed the advice of the *expert*. But we had the best experience in the third restaurant, when we followed the *swarm*—the locals and our own instincts—to the little corner restaurant. Combining these three input sources—the crowd, the experts, and the swarm—forms the foundation of the coolhunting process. Following the crowd tells us the big trends. Following the experts tells us the subtleties of the trend. And following the swarm tells us what's really going to be cool.

On the Internet, buzz corresponds and directly mirrors the trends from the real world. On the Web, we have perfect access to the real world for crowds, experts, and swarms. The Web at large, and what's said on the online editions of large newspapers such as the *New York*

Times and *Wall Street Journal*, tells us what the crowd thinks about a certain subject. We can easily get these news items using search engines such as Google or Yahoo.

To get the opinion of the experts, we can ask the blogs. Every expert with some professional pride is maintaining a personal blog these days. Individual experts might be wrong—author Nassim Taleb once said that experts are right 50 percent of the time, only we never know in which 50 percent we are—but from a collection of expert predictions we can hope to get greater accuracy.

To get the wisdom of the swarm, we can ask online forums. Patient forums, for example, have become platforms of information exchange for patients with a rare disease; investor forums bustle with small-scale investors sharing trading tips; movie forums are full of movie buffs. There is literally no limit to the different types of forums that exist online. Combining the wisdom of crowds on the Web, the wisdom of experts through blogs, and the wisdom of swarms through online forums generates surprisingly accurate predictions about what people believe is going to happen. Table 7–1 illustrates this process for the examples of soccer, stock prices, and new products in general.

Table 7-1. Coolhunting for soccer results, bargain stocks, and cool new products through analyzing the wisdom of crowds, experts, and swarms.

	Soccer	Influence Outcome	Stock	Influence Outcome	New Product	Influence Outcome
Crowd	Audience	Cheer better, louder	Potential investors	Talk well, buy stock	Potential buyers	Talk well, buy products (Web)
Expert	Coach, referee	Coach, judge better	Financial analyst, journalist	Talk well, recommend stock	Market analysts	Recommend product (news blogs)
Swarm	Soccer team	Play better	Employees, shareholders	Work better	Employees, customers	Product (online forums)

To predict the outcome of a soccer game, we need to combine our readings of the audience, the coach, and the soccer team. The audience forms the crowd; the more it cheers, the better the team supposedly will play. The influence of the audience is only marginal for the outcome of the game. The quality of the coach matters far more. At least that's what soccer club presidents think; that's why they make an investment by hiring the best coaches. The biggest influence on the outcome of the soccer game, however, is the team itself, or the swarm. Club presidents must think the same, since star players usually command much higher salaries than star coaches.

The same combination of the wisdom of the crowd, the experts, and the swarm also determines the stock price of a company. If the potential investors—the crowd—think highly of the company, they will drive up the stock price. The financial analysts and journalists—the experts—also are able to influence the stock price. Collectively, they can manipulate the stock price through buy or sell recommendations. But the biggest influence on the stock price comes from the employees of the company—the swarm. If they work well, the company will do well. We can read what they think in company forums, or even internal e-mail archives.

The trick for our web-based coolhunting is to emulate this process through scouring the Web and reading the online minds of the crowd, the experts, and the swarm. If we had a chance to get access to the corporate e-mail archives of companies and compare the communication structure among the employees of the company, it would tell us a lot about how well the company operates. If we would find highly collaborative teams, COINs, this finding would predict future success and high performance of the company. Most companies until now have been unwilling to share this data with researchers. In our MIT projects, however, we have been fortunate to collaborate with dozens of companies where we have had the opportunity to analyze many communication archives, looking at e-mails, blog traffic, and online forums. In some of our most recent projects we even used social badges, invented at the MIT Media Lab by Sandy Pentland and his graduate students, to measure face-to-face interaction among people. Using sensors to evaluate communication and interaction on the microscopic level permits us to capture who talks to whom, who looks at whom, and who is excited or bored, and to collect this information continuously over extended periods of time.

However these interaction archives are collected, analyzing the communication of teams of knowledge workers has allowed us to find the COINs, the stars, and the galaxies among those knowledge workers. Communication in COIN-like structures, growing to become CLNs and CINs, turns out to be a strong predictor of success. The more people communicate, the more successful they are.[1]

Unfortunately, for new product or stock trend analysis these communication archives of organizations are not readily available. We therefore need to find other publicly accessible communication archives to read the minds of crowds, experts, and swarms. Luckily, the Web provides us with a vast repository of just such information. We can find the opinion of the crowd through combing the Web with clever search engine queries. We can find the opinion of the experts by automatically mining investment research websites, news sites, and investor blogs. And we can find the opinion of the swarm on online investor forums such as Yahoo Finance, Raging Bull, or Motley Fool. Using and combining these different data sources, we can make predictions about the future success of a company at a surprisingly accurate rate.[2]

The last column in Table 7–1 describes a generic case of how the success of a new product is influenced by the crowd, the experts, and the swarm. Reading the minds of buyers of a new product on the Web gives a first indication of future success, based on the collective and aggregated opinion of the crowd. Reading the online mind of bloggers, by analyzing what blogs have to say about a new product, is another indication of the perception of this new product in the market. As every venture capitalist knows, the best prediction of the success of a new product can be made by looking at the team behind it. Unfortunately, corporate e-mail archives are not readily available, so this analysis cannot easily be done. However, the opinion of customers of the new product—the swarm—can be gauged by tracking their discussion in online forums. Combining analysis of all three sources—crowds, experts, and swarms—will therefore give a pretty good picture about where the new product likely will be headed.

Over the last five years researchers at MIT and Dartmouth College have built a software tool called Condor[3] that monitors activity on the Web in order to analyze and predict large-scale trends such as the future of stock prices and election results. Condor has successfully predicted the results of the 2008 U.S. presidential election, an Italian political party's internal election and the subsequent national political election in 2008, as well as stock market fluctuations and who will win an Oscar.

To understand how Condor works, let's look how it measures buzz on the Web for a certain subject. Condor starts by taking a search term, such as the name of a political candidate or a company, and running it through a Google, Bing, or Yahoo search. Condor then takes the web links of the top search results and plugs them into the search field, prefaced with the term "link." The search engine then returns the sites that link to the original sites, which Condor then reinserts into the search engine. Condor maps the links between all the sites it has found, even if they do not contain the original search term, and finds the shortest way to get from one site to the other through the links they contain. The more often a site is involved in moving between sites, the higher its centrality score. Condor averages the centrality scores for all of the sites to produce an overall score for the original search term. The score provides an indication of the popularity of what has been searched.

This system works not only for web queries, but also for blogs and online forums. In this case we again construct the social network—this time not of web sites, but of the bloggers, or the people posting on the online forum about the subject. By linking to each other's posts, bloggers provide a vote of confidence for another blogger's post. Combining all of these links again permits the system to extract the most central blog posts. For online forums, the speed and frequency with which other posters respond to a new post is a measure of importance for a given post. For example, in December 2006, we used this system to compare a range of film titles from that year. A group of students in a course I was teaching analyzed the communication in the online forum of the Internet Movie Database, IMDB.com. Of the eight movies that scored highest in their prediction system, five won Oscars, two others were nominated, and only one did not receive an award or a nomination.[4]

Another of our methods of coolhunting is mining people's e-mails, which immediately raises red flags of privacy to many people. However, we have worked out the ethics for disclosure for this kind of activity. Over the last six years we have analyzed many organizational e-mail archives such as the Deloitte Consulting e-mail archive (described in Chapter 6). To overcome the initial reluctance of people to expose the contents of their mailbox, we have developed a set of guidelines. In our research projects, we only share individual insights with each concerned individual, but not the person's boss. In corporate projects, policies on protection of privacy rest with the organization and depend on local laws, which differ. In the United States, people can opt out of such projects; in Europe, they have to opt in. Before we start a project, we do our best to openly inform project participants about goals, the policies and procedures applied, and most important, what's in it for them. In past projects, we have looked at communication among members of a marketing team at a bank, at engineers at a Detroit car company, at researchers in an Italian research lab, at executives in a European global high-tech company, and at nurses in a Boston hospital, to name just a few.

Let's now look at some concrete examples to better understand how Condor can be used to predict cool trends by finding the trendsetters.

Coolhunting U.S. Presidential Candidates

In May 2008, the battle among U.S. presidential candidates still was a three-way fight between Hillary Clinton, Barack Obama, and John McCain. On May 5, the pastor of the predominantly black church where Obama was a member, Jeremiah Wright, made inflammatory remarks about the relationships between blacks and whites in the United States. His remarks found immediate reflection in the Coolhunting Blog buzz scores of the three presidential candidates that same morning (see Figure 7–2), with things turning especially bad for Barack Obama. As can be seen in the centrality score the following day, the damage done by the inciting remarks of his pastor undermined Obama's standing in the blogosphere. His score (in light gray) had never been as low since we started tracking him in March 2008. While scores of all three candidates went down, in relative terms, Hillary Clinton seemed to rebound (dark gray).

At the same time, the buzz on the Web seemed to indicate that the damage was not so bad after all: Obama still was leading (as he was in the polls in the "real world"), but because blogs point the way of things to come, this was a real wake-up call for Obama to distance himself from his confrontational pastor—which he subsequently did.

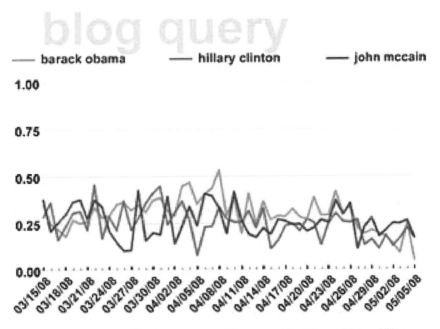

FIGURE 7–2. Coolhunting Blog buzz scores of three presidential candidates: Hillary Clinton, Barack Obama, and John McCain (May 5, 2008).

How are these buzz scores calculated? Figure 7–3 illustrates how the centrality of each of the candidates is measured through the social network built up through the links obtained by the search engine queries (as described in the previous section). On March 29, 2008, Obama and McCain each had a buzz share of 40 percent, while Clinton's was 20 percent. Repeating this process every day leads to curves such as those shown in Figure 7–2 and also Figure 7–4, which depicts the buzz score curve from March 2008 to the end of May 2008.

While Hillary Clinton had not yet conceded defeat (which she did three days later on June 3), it is quite obvious from the buzz level that, at least on the Web, her stardom could not keep up with the charisma of Barack Obama. Her buzz score already had predicted future defeat three months earlier. On the other hand, the coolhunting scores also nicely illustrate how the prolonged fight between Clinton and Obama hurt the Democratic candidates. John McCain won the Republican

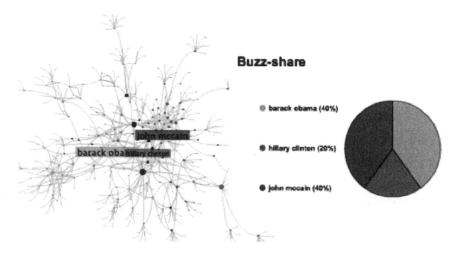

FIGURE 7–3. Social network of websites talking about Barack Obama, Hillary Clinton, and John McCain (March 29, 2008).

nomination in early March; soon thereafter his Web score jumped, as the sharp rise in the black line around March 22 shows in Figure 7–4. Barack Obama's score stayed more or less on the same level, occasionally dipping and rebounding, but certainly not rising, while Hillary Clinton's fortunes were declining.

Polls about U.S. presidential elections are notoriously inaccurate, but our Condor-based coolhunting tool that monitors the Web offers a much faster and cheaper way to obtain the same information. For most of the first six months of 2008, Barack Obama had been leading his competitor, John McCain, in the polls by three to six percentage points. This is far less than the fifteen points by which the Democrats had been leading the Republicans in the polls for the senatorial elections.

According to many analysts, one hidden reason for the single-digit lead of Obama was the issue of race. This is a delicate subject that Americans seem afraid to admit in public and therefore lie about to the pollster, similar to how people lie when asked about going to church, exercising, and drinking alcohol. When asked in person whether they go to church regularly, 56 percent answered yes. When asked anonymously, only 25 percent described themselves as regular churchgoers. When personally asked if they exercised regularly, 58 percent claimed they did. When asked anonymously, this number dropped to 35 percent. When asked about drinking alcohol regularly, anonymous answers resulted in 53 percent of people regularly consuming alcohol; when personally asked, only 39 percent admitted to drinking regularly.

This inconsistency in answering polling questions leads one to wonder if people were not telling the truth about planning to vote for a black president. It seems that our web-based coolhunting system can provide a more honest answer. Doing a coolhunt comparing the buzz surrounding John McCain with the buzz about Barack Obama from August 7 to August 18, 2008, tells a story that is quite different from the polls.

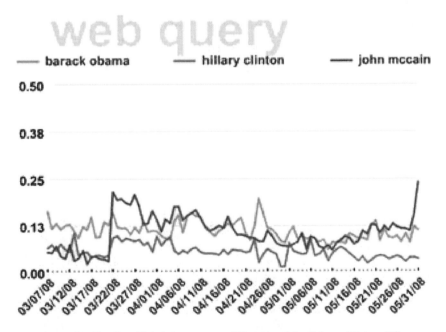

FIGURE 7–4. Coolhunting Web buzz scores of three presidential candidates: Hillary Clinton, Barack Obama, and John McCain (May 31, 2008).

As Figure 7–5 shows, it did not look good for Barack Obama, at least on the Web. The websites talking about John McCain carried greater weight than the sites talking about Barack Obama. McCain's websites were better linked than the ones talking about Obama. The difference is slight, but as we know, in the U.S. presidential elections sometimes a slight difference can make all the difference. Which is telling the truth—the Web or the polls? In our observations, the Web frequently predicted what was going to happen later in the polls and elections. And indeed, in late summer of 2008, McCain gained the lead in the polls over Obama until the deepening financial crisis turned the wheel of fortune again in favor of Obama.

Figure 7–6 illustrates the Blog buzz on the day of the U.S. presidential election, November 4, 2008. Democrat Barack Obama won the election against Republican John McCain with a landslide in electoral votes (365 against McCain's 173) and 53 percent of the popular vote. The upper left window in Figure 7–6 shows the readings that changed by the minute, based on new posts on important blogs such as HuffingtonPost.com or PowerLineBlog.com. However, the overall trend favoring Obama (the black line) can

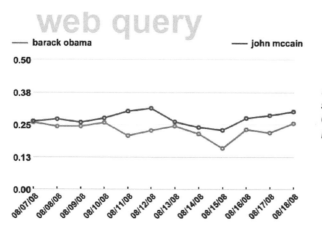

FIGURE 7–5. Web buzz surrounding Barack Obama and John McCain (August 2008).

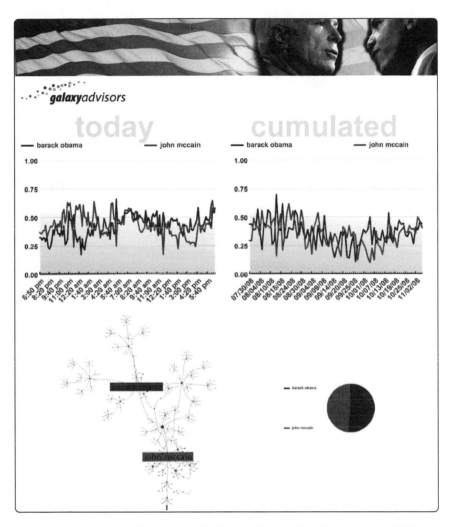

FIGURE 7–6. Blog buzz of Obama and McCain on Election Day (November 4, 2008).

clearly be seen. In the accumulated graph, the upper right window of Figure 7–6, starting in September, Obama's blog buzz level consistently trumped McCain's buzz.

In Figure 7–6, too, the bottom left picture shows the social network of blog posts. The blogs talking about McCain form a far more compact cluster, at the very bottom with a tightly interlinked structure. The Democratic blogs, linking to Obama, are much more widely spread out, and also exhibit fewer interconnecting links, reflecting the wider political interests of the voters supporting Obama. The pie chart at the lower right shows the relative importance of the two candidates, 53 percent for Obama, against 47 percent for McCain. Note that this relative importance corresponded to the exact percentages for the candidates in the popular vote.

Coolhunting the Value of Brands: Looking for the End of the Federer Era

In another coolhunting project we looked at the buzz surrounding the world's best tennis players in the summer of 2008. We compared the hype surrounding the longtime number-two player, Rafael Nadal, and then number-one Roger Federer. When we started our coolhunting, Nadal was on the verge of taking over the number-one spot from Federer. After Federer lost two epic battles against Nadal in Paris and Wimbledon in June and early July of 2008, Nadal was poised to switch positions with Federer on August 18, and become seeded world number one.

As you would expect, Nadal was ahead of Federer according to Web buzz (Figure 7–7) for the first eleven days. Federer then shortly beat Nadal's buzz when the Olympics began, where he was hugely popular and (like Nadal) a top contender for the Gold medal—until he lost in the quarterfinals on August 13 against James Blake. Afterward, Nadal took over again until August 17, where the impending transfer of the crown from Federer to Nadal brought increased buzz levels to both.

It had been a masterful four and a half years for Roger Federer, which came to a close in the middle of August 2008. But at least in Web buzz, he could more than keep up during the transition from being number one to number two. These curves were coming not from any polls, but simply from analyzing which websites talked about Federer

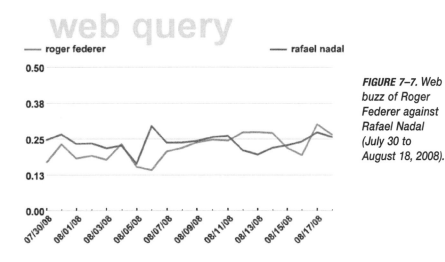

FIGURE 7–7. Web buzz of Roger Federer against Rafael Nadal (July 30 to August 18, 2008).

or Nadal, and weighting those sites by "votes" from other websites pointing to them through web links. What this means is that although Federer had to give up the title of the top-seeded player to Rafael Nadal, the value of his brand (for example, to potential sponsors) remained unabashedly high—good news for Roger Federer, indeed.

Why the World's Most Influential Intellectual Is an Islamic Cleric

During the first half of 2008 over a half million people voted over the Internet to find out the world's top intellectuals in a vote organized by the U.K. magazines *Prospect* and *Foreign Policy*. The goal was to come up with rankings of the top-100 living intellectuals. This was a rerun of a 2005 campaign that had concluded that Noam Chomsky and Umberto Eco were the most influential intellectuals.

This time, early leaders were Mario Vargas Llosa, Gary Kasparov, and Al Gore. But then a campaign was organized for the Turkish Islamist preacher Fethullah Gülen, leading him to a resounding victory as the world's most influential intellectual.

According to *Prospect*, the leading Turkish newspaper *Zaman*, with a circulation of more than 700,000, succeeded in rallying its readers behind Fethullah Gülen. However, other newspapers in Indonesia, Bulgaria, or Malaysia launched similar campaigns, with little success.

Here are the top-12 intellectuals according to *Foreign Policy/ Prospect* (in parenthesis is the person's ranking in 2005, with an asterisk if they did not appear in the 2005 ranking at all):

1. Fethullah Gülen (*)

2. Muhammad Yunus (*)

3. Yusuf Al-Qaradawi (56)

4. Orhan Pamuk (54)

5. Aitzaz Ahsan (*)

6. Amr Khaled (*)

7. Abdolkarim Soroush (15)

8. Tariq Ramadan (58)

9. Mahmood Mamdani (*)

10. Shirin Ebadi (12)

11. Noam Chomsky (1)

12. Al Gore (*)

When these rankings were picked up by the Western press, claims were made that the campaign did not reflect the real world. We therefore looked at what coolhunting with Condor would tell us. Here, in Figures 7–8 and 7–9, is the resulting picture, only comparing a subset of five intellectuals.

Amazingly, our coolhunting tool pretty much confirmed the rankings in the *Foreign Policy/Prospect* 2008 poll,[5] although we initially only

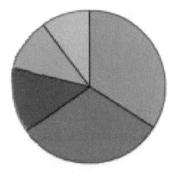

Fethullah Gulen (34%)

Muhammad Yunus (31%)

Yusuf Al-Qaradawi (14%)

Noam Chomsky (11%)

Al Gore (10%)

FIGURE 7–8. Rankings of five of world's most influential intellectuals.

checked for five people out of the 100 public figures. None of the top websites "voting" for Fethullah Gülen was a Zaman news site. So it could well be that the *Foreign Policy/Prospect* poll indeed mirrored global intellectual influence, as the Internet is being used more and more actively in developing countries, where a large fraction of the population is Muslim, or at least likes to take the opportunity to literally kick in the shin of Uncle Sam. We then later also

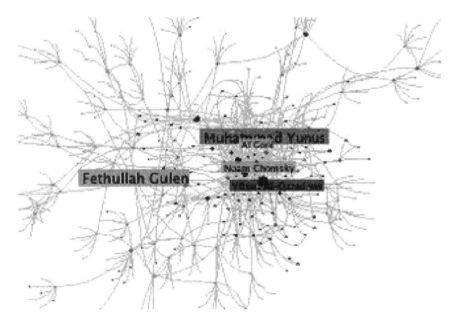

FIGURE 7–9. Spiderweb of sites that "voted" Fethullah Gülen to victory as world's most influential intellectual.

did a detailed coolhunting for all 100 intellectuals, with yielded rankings somewhat different from the *Foreign Policy/Prospect* poll, where German philosopher Jürgen Habermas got the leading spot, followed by Fethullah Gülen. Figure 7–10 illustrates the tangled web of relationships among the intellectuals, which makes it nearly impossible to track individual connections, but permits us to measure the importance of each intellectual.

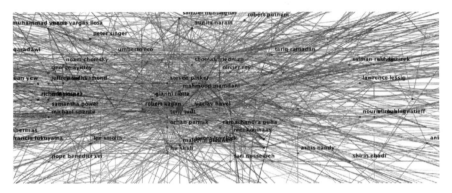

FIGURE 7–10. *Social network on the Web of world's top-100 leading intellectuals.*

But this could also be because we did this coolhunt about one month after the online voting was concluded, and as we have seen before, the collective mind of the crowd is a fickle thing, which can change in an instant.

Predicting the Outcome of the Academy Awards

Besides predicting the strengths of brands and where political elections are heading, we have also successfully forecast the outcome of the Academy Awards. For the 2007 Oscars, a team of students at the University of Cologne analyzed the Internet Movie Database (IMDB). In particular, we looked at the intensity of buzz in the online Oscar forum, where people talk about which actors, directors, and movies might win an Oscar.

The students also examined the general discussion in the "Reviews and Previews" forum, to predict how much money a movie might generate at the box office. They developed their own method where they constructed a social network of people based on what volume of responses a person posting on the forum generated. If somebody's post elicited many responses, the person who was posting became central in the social network. The students then combined the social network position of the poster with what posters said, and whether they spoke positively or negatively about a certain movie title. A comment such as, "I think *Pirates of the Caribbean* is a great movie," for example, would count positively for the opening-day box-office prediction for that movie.

Looking at the changes in what people said on the IMDB forum, in positive or negative words, combined with their social network position as an approximation of their influence, allowed us to correctly predict how much money a movie would make, one week before the movie was officially shown for the first time.

Applying the same concept to predict if a movie would be awarded an Oscar, the students made nine predictions for Oscars out of the twenty-five movies discussed the most in the IMDB Oscar online forum. Their clear front-runner for an Oscar was *The Departed*, which indeed won four Oscars. Among their other eight predictions, four won an Oscar, and three others were nominated for an Oscar. Note that these predictions were made more than a month before the Oscars nominations were announced. In addition, the intensity of the buzz about the movie also corresponded to the "quality" of the Oscars obtained, with *The Departed*, winner of Best Picture and Best Director awards and two "lesser" Oscars, generating much more buzz than *Little Miss Sunshine*, which garnered two Oscars for Best Screenplay and Best Supporting Actor. This corresponds very well to the real-world ranking among the different Oscars, where Best Picture carries much more prestige than Best Supporting Actor.

Predicting Stock Trends

The same method of predicting the outcome of elections, of winning Oscars, and of how much money a movie will be making at box office on opening day can also be used to predict stock prices.

In particular, we compared the changes in buzz—in investor forums such as Yahoo Finance, on blogs, and on the Internet—with the changes in the stock price. Figure 7–11 illustrates the correlation between the fluctuation in Web and blog buzz and the fluctuation in the IBM stock price. Through use of sophisticated matching algorithms, dynamically combining the discussion in the forums with the amount of buzz on blogs and on the Web, we obtained almost parallel curves far above what pure chance would have given us.

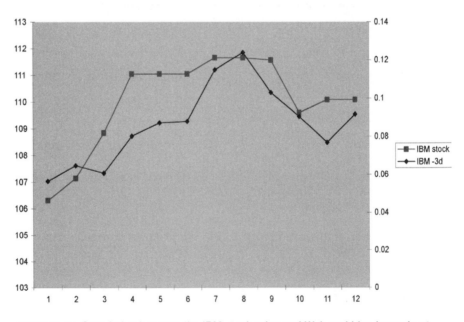

FIGURE 7–11. Correlation between the IBM stock price and Web and blog buzz about IBM. Note: Gray line is stock price over twelve days; black line is intensity of Web buzz over the same time period.

Predicting the Actions of People Using Social Badges

Sandy Pentland, a professor at the MIT Media Lab, has been developing jointly with his graduate students a series of "social microscopes" that he calls "social badges." The social badges (shown in Figure 7–12) combine a Bluetooth sensor to measure the relative locations of the wearer, an infrared sensor that analyzes if people wearing the badges are facing each other, an accelerometer that measures how excited the people wearing the badges are, and a microphone that measures the pitch of the voice of the wearer, as a further indicator of the level of excitement.

Using these badges, Sandy and his students have been able to predict if people were paying attention to the speaker in meetings, and in speed-dating situations, if the two people would end up exchanging phone numbers. Together with Sandy and his students, we used these social badges to identify social interaction networks on a much more granular and interpersonal level than by just mining e-mail, blogs, and online forums. In particular, we analyzed the interaction of twenty employees at a German bank, as well as the interaction among nurses in a Boston area teaching hospital.

In the German bank, twenty members of the marketing department wore the badges for the duration of one month. Collecting the interaction data from the badges, and comparing it with the social network constructed from e-mails already exchanged, showed us that different people were central to the e-mail and the face-to-face interaction networks. For example, the department head was very central in the face-to-face social network; obviously he was a "floor-walker," someone who was talking personally and continuously with the members of his group. On the other hand, the department secretary was quite peripheral in the face-to-face network, but very central to the e-mail network.

But more interesting things can be found out by combining the face-to-face and e-mail social networks. Interpreting the readings of the social badges allowed us to predict if people were introverts or extroverts, if they were neurotic, if they were agreeable, and if they were open for new things. Combining the readings on the team level for five different teams also allowed us to find the creative and not-so-creative teams.[6] This was very valuable for the bank, as some of the teams, such as the one developing new marketing campaigns, were looking for creative people, while the team giving phone support didn't particularly need creativity, but rather agreeable people.

FIGURE 7–12. Social badge.

We also found some people who had quite important roles as communicators, but, as it turned out, spent most of their time tucked away in their offices. Based on our findings, the bank was therefore able to realign people based on their real strengths and weaknesses. Another interesting finding was that the most extroverted people had a hard time finding discussion partners, whereas introverts and moderately extroverted people were much more likely to be chosen for a chat.

We repeated this experiment in a different setting, in the Post-Anesthesia Care Unit (PACU) in a Boston area hospital. The PACU in this hospital gets up to eighty patients wheeled in from the operation rooms every day. These patients are then cared for by about a dozen nurses until they have regained consciousness and can be brought to their rooms. For the duration of one month, sixty-nine nurses, nurse assistants, anesthesiologists, and residents were wearing our social badges. One of our first findings was that besides the nurse director and the nurse team leaders, there were some senior nurses who had no official senior role, but were very central to the successful operation of the PACU.

One of our goals was to find ways of reducing stress for the people working in the pressure-cooker environment of the PACU. We asked them every day about the level of stress they felt, how efficient they thought they had been, and how happy they felt at the end of the day. It turned out that the more people were actually facing each other, the less stressed they felt. This means that simply talking to one another can take away workers' stress. The crucial point, however, is that the other person also needs to face the speaker. When we just counted the sheer number of interactions with other people where there was no reciprocity, people felt more stressed the more they spoke. On the other hand, the nurses also felt more productive on days when they spoke a lot. Our recommendation: Take the time to listen and talk to other people on an individual level and look at them while you talk. This will reduce stress. But we also recommended that the hospital design tasks and room layout to reduce involuntary interaction among larger groups of people, in particular in a high-interaction, high-stress environment such as the PACU. This also will help reduce stress.

We also wanted to find out if there were ways of making the PACU function more efficiently. We therefore measured the average delay times of getting recovered patients to their rooms. It turned out that on days where the PACU was operating more hierarchically—with a few senior people in charge—it was operating more efficiently. This clearly illustrates the difference between communication in a marketing team, where creativity is at a premium, and a high-throughput environment like the PACU. For creative tasks, communication in a decentralized, direct way is best, but for high-throughput tasks, hierarchical communication with a few people in charge is better.

We are barely one year into this new line of research. Exploration of these social microscopes is at the early stages, and we expect to gain many more insights for personal and team-level productivity and creativity. In a new book, *Honest Signals: How They Shape Our World*,[7] Sandy Pentland is mapping out a wide range of applications where social badges might give us new insights not possible before.

After looking at this practical application of the coolfarming process for discovering, measuring, and predicting trends through finding the creative people, the final chapter will now try to answer the one fundamental question we have not tackled before. Why are people willing to give up individual benefits for the sake of the COIN and become coolfarmers?

8

What Motivates Coolfarmers?

Unus pro omnibus—omnes pro uno: "One for all—all for one."

WHAT MOTIVATES people to coolfarm? Why do people want to start a new trend? Why do people join a COIN? Why are people interested in learning about the products of a COIN? Why do they buy into the goals of a COIN, thus helping to get a new trend over the tipping point? These key questions are at the very heart of coolfarming.

Let's start by hearing what one of our great role models of coolfarming, Linus Torvalds, has to say about this subject. In an interview, he said that his motivational factors are "fun," "fame," and "feeling good." According to Torvalds, "Most good programmers do programming not because they expect to get paid, or because they expect admiration by the public, but because it is fun to program."[1] What this means is that they love what they are doing. Their motivation comes from the intrinsic joy of doing their favorite activity, of getting "in flow" with their environment and with what they do. Of course, because they are good at what they do, they also become admired by the public, which gets them to work even harder. Only they do not see this as hard work, but as fun, and the most meaningful use of their active time.

In the future, Torvalds thinks that people will be motivated by three factors: "survival," "social life," and "entertainment." Joining a COIN is normally not done for survival, but for "entertainment"—or, in Torvalds's sense of the word, for finding meaning and purpose in life. Entertainment doesn't just mean playing computer games; it also encompasses quite serious endeavors, like working out a way of going to the moon. To be together with other like-minded souls also includes the second motivational factor of Linus Torvalds, the "social life." Working together with others to create something new as a group plays a fundamental motivational role for COIN members.

Coolfarmers Show Yhteisöllisyys and Gemeinsinn

To study why and how we like to create new things in groups, let's look at the Finns, not just because this is where Linus Torvalds comes from, but also because Finns like to do everything in groups. Finland is a small nation that has been extremely successful. In the last thirty years it has become one of the wealthiest and best-educated countries in the world. Studying why the Finns work in groups allows us to answer the fundamental question: "What are the genes that are the most successful for the survival and growth of the hive?" Hives of naturally homogenous members make good testing grounds to study how new swarms are born.

The Finns are among the most wired people on earth, as well as quite homogeneous, most likely due to their native language, which is only spoken by Finns, and their geographic position, at the northern border of Europe. They are eager users of blogging and social networking. They were among the early adopters of LinkedIn, and they have enthusiastically embraced other social networking tools like Facebook. They even coined a new term—"Yhteisöllisyys"—that refers to people who buy tech gadgets to obtain the right to belong to their own self-chosen digital tribe. "Yhteisöllisyys" comes from the term *yhteisö*, which means "community" or "society" in Finnish. But as was explained to me, Yhteisöllisyys is more than just the Finnish word for community. It stands for the propensity of people to form communities. These Finnish communities are self-selected groups of people who get part of their meaning of life from belonging to virtual communities sharing the same passion, be it for soccer or for a high-tech gadget.

It is not enough do be part of a virtual community. What counts is to be a passionate member of the virtual community. Surprisingly often, what Finns are passionate about becomes a trend very soon thereafter in the rest of Europe or in the United States. When I was trying to find a concise translation for Yhteisöllisyys, my Finnish friends struggled and ended up suggesting "communality," immediately adding, however, that even this word does not really translate the concept well. It seems there is no real translation, but the point is clear: Finns like to do everything in groups, and intrasociety trust is huge.

When I am in a restaurant with Finnish friends, I never cease to be amazed by the habit of Finnish restaurant owners to accept a business card instead of a credit card when the time comes to pay the bill. The restaurant will then just send an invoice to the business card owner. This level of trust for a stranger—although one who moves within the community of Finns—would be unimaginable in most other places. Because of Yhteisöllisyys, Finns strive to be members in good standing of their chosen tribe. To remain in good standing, they will behave well—which means paying up on their obligations to the restaurant owner, for example.

In German, there is also a word that describes obligations toward society—*Gemeinsinn*. It means to have public spirit. People with Gemeinsinn put the community's benefit before their own—just like the bees behave. To be successful members of a community, people

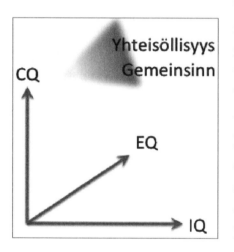

FIGURE 8–1. From IQ to CQ.

with Gemeinsinn need not only intelligence (IQ) and emotional intelligence (EQ), but also "group smarts." COIN members, too, therefore have this third form of intelligence, or collective intelligence (CQ), which captures our capability of being smart as a member of a group. CQ is different from EQ (see Figure 8–1). CQ includes character traits such as the willingness to delegate authority to the group, to stand behind your own opinion while being ready to accept the opinions of others, to demonstrate fairness in dealing with others, and to accept and give constructive criticism.

For an example of how Yhteisöllisyys and Gemeinsinn benefit a community, compare the attitudes of southern Italy and Switzerland on the subject of trash removal. The city of Naples has been drowning in garbage for the last thirty years, while Switzerland has a reputation for being extremely clean. In Italy, in particular in the south, all trust goes to the family, while trust in society is very low. Noted scholar Francis Fukuyama has called this phenomenon "Italian Confucianism."[2] The city of Naples has thirty quarters (or neighbor-hoods), and one quarter seems unwilling to accept the trash of another quarter. "Everybody for him- or herself!" seems to be the motto. And anyone could see, feel, and smell the consequences all across Naples in 2007. Heaps of garbage piled up because no quarter was willing to be the garbage dump of the city, or even the local neighborhood. Pollution in southern Italy was so bad that one of the main exports, mozzarella cheese made from the milk of domestic buffalo, became poisoned when the grass the buffalo were eating became contaminated with garbage, too. As a consequence of this egoistic attitude, mozzarella could not be sold abroad.

Compare the situation in Naples with Switzerland, which is most of the time—as clean as it gets. Swiss children are taught at school that you inconvenience others if you throw trash on the street—you violate Gemeinsinn, and you are expected to share the environment with the community. When people just throw away their chewing gum or candy bar wrap for their own convenience, they mess up the environment for everybody. I also have noticed the same attitude toward cleanliness in Helsinki, Finland, where an army of little street sweeping cars is brushing the streets every morning with water. The end effect is a cleaner and healthier environment for all to enjoy. Gemeinsinn benefits everybody, including those engag-ing in "Gemeinsinn."

We don't have to go far to find role models for this sort of com-munity-oriented, even community-immersed, behavior in the business world. Large companies like Apple, Nike, and Cisco are trying to be well-behaved corporate world citizens. For an individual and highly successful example, look at Oprah Winfrey. Oprah's Book Club works well because she does not take any money for her recommendations.

Rather, she tries to recommend what she thinks is good for her readers. She does not suggest what is good for the author, the publisher, or herself (by getting a cut from the author or publisher), but what benefits her audience. Of course, what is good for the readers will be good also for the author and the publisher, driving up sales. And in the end, this is also good for Oprah, because it builds her brand as an impartial judge of books of high quality to improve the general taste and knowledge of the American public.

Basing your business model on the principles of Yhteisöllisyys and Gemeinsinn improves the world for all stakeholders, not just the business owner but also employees and customers. For example, Apple stores defy conventional retail wisdom by paying their sales staff a fixed salary, with stellar results for Apple. With the pressure to sell taken away, Apple store employees have a more relaxed and customer-friendly attitude, greatly increasing the buying experience of clients, which leads to Apple stores being the most profitable stores, per square meter, in the United States, at double the level of profitability as their nearest competitor. Swarm businesses based on Yhteisöllisyys and Gemeinsinn can be very profitable.

Coolfarmers Are Ethical

Successful coolfarmers adhere to a strict ethical code. The work ethic of exemplary coolfarmers, such as open-source programmers, is quite different from the Protestant work ethic as defined by German sociologist Max Weber, who saw it as the obligation of each member of society to work as hard and dutifully as possible to please God. The work ethic of an open-source programmer, by comparison, includes flexible working hours, creativity, and a passion for one's own work. This ethic also disdains monetary reward for one's achievements, preferring what the open-source programmers call Egoboo—the respect of their peers.

The main reason this work ethic based on a self-organizing way of developing new things works so well can be described in one word—*transparency*. Computers, the Internet, blogs, wikis, and social networking sites are enablers of transparency. In the early Internet days, a famous *New Yorker* cartoon showed a dog sitting at a computer telling another dog, "On the Internet, nobody knows you're a dog." This has totally changed as today's web society has introduced total transparency.

In a media-dominated world, people gaming the system get exposed much faster, leading to a new definition of ethical behavior. Fifty years ago, the late Kenneth Lay, former Enron CEO, might have gone into the history books not as a corporate villain, but as a hero and founder of a highly innovative company. But this sort of behavior does not go undetected and unpunished anymore. The e-mail communication of Enron clearly demonstrated that Ken Lay was well informed about the unethical behavior of key people in his company, counter to his own words and the printed Enron code of ethics.[3] Today's leaders are expected to not just verbally declare but personally demonstrate ethical behavior, and to treat their stakeholders in an ethical way.

Ethical behavior not only avoids punishment, but also brings handsome rewards. As a company, it pays to be ethical in dealing with customers, employees, and suppliers. Remi Trudel and June Cotte from the University of Western Ontario investigated whether people were willing to pay more for ethically produced goods.[4] What they found in a series of experiments was that people were willing to pay premiums for coffee and cotton T-shirts if they knew that the producers were compensated fairly and the ingredients were produced in a "green" way.

In particular, Trudel and Cotte defined ethical business behavior as having good relations with all stakeholders, including consumers, and making sure that employees were hired and paid fairly, that the production process was run in an ethical way, that the raw materials were ecofriendly, and that human rights were respected and no child labor was used in overseas factories. While consumers paid a 10 percent to 15 percent premium for ethically produced coffee, they punished unethical producers by asking for a 20 percent discount for unethically produced goods compared to the generic price for the same good. People with especially high ethical expectations were willing to pay another 20 percent premium for ethically produced coffee, compared to average consumers.

The conclusion for leaders of COINs is that they have no choice but to behave in an ethical way. If they do so, they will be rewarded with a high-functioning COIN. If they try to do otherwise, their COIN members will punish them with their feet, walking away from the COIN. The case of a senior editor of Wikipedia illustrates what happens when a member breaks the ethical code of the COIN.

COINs Need Cops

In the beehive there are the guard bees, looking out for law and order. They keep intruders out, and even sacrifice themselves if needed to protect their swarm. A similar role exists also in human swarms, where some COIN members make sure that Collaborative Innovation Networks work together on high ethical standards. Like bees, human swarms are more successful in coolfarming new trends if they have the self-appointed "cops" making sure that all COIN members adhere to the ethical code.

It's not a good idea to abuse virtual trust. If this happens, the cops in the COIN turn to action. Take the following example. Some time ago there was big turmoil among Wikipedia contributors about the fake identity of "essjay." As the *New York Times* reported, a very active Wikipedian with the screen name of "essjay" had edited thousands of articles, pretending to be a tenured professor of religion at a private university, while in fact he was a twenty-four-year-old who had attended a number of colleges.

The revolt was not so much about essjay pretending to be somebody else. Rather, what the Wikipedia community did not tolerate was essjay using the moral authority of his assumed faculty position in disputes about the content of the articles he was editing. For example, defending an editing decision, essjay had written, "This is a text I often require for my students, and I would hang my own PhD on its credibility." This, unfortunately, was too much for the Wikipedian community to accept, and so essjay in effect hanged himself by his fake identity and was forced to resign.

The lesson is simple: Don't pretend to be more than you are, at least not on the Web, because transparency in the online community will bring out the truth, and usually sooner rather than later. (It is no longer true that "on the Internet, nobody knows you're a dog.") Essjay had broken the ethical code of Wikipedians, and so he had to pay the ultimate price—he was forced to leave his self-chosen online community. But this case still begs the question: "Why had essjay gone to all the trouble of investing so much time and effort to create his virtual identity?" The answer is simple: He wanted to be a well-respected, even a leading member of his community. But it's not a good idea to try to reach this goal by lying, certainly not in a COIN.

Fortunately, there is good news for members in good standing of a COIN. If we are a well-behaved member of a COIN, adhering to its ethical code, this behavior will make us happier.

Coolfarmers Are Happy

We all like to be happy, and COIN members and coolfarmers are no exception. So the question is: What makes us happy? Happiness researcher Bruno S. Frey[5] found that the activities that make us the happiest are those that involve being with friends, which on average we tend to do for two hours a day. Activities that make us the unhappiest are being with our boss, which on average we do for two and a half hours per day; doing housework, done for one hour per day; working, done for seven hours per day; and commuting, which we do for one hour and forty minutes per day, on average.

COIN members are in a really good situation, since they are able to tailor their day for optimized happiness: In an ordinary nine-to-five job, we have very little control over who our colleagues and our boss are. COIN members are much more fortunate. As they self-select and self-organize their work and role, they choose their team and their boss. They therefore have happy hours at work and with their boss. And if they work virtually, in cyberteams, they have no need for commuting. Most likely, they consider their COIN colleagues to be friends as well, which makes interaction with them a pleasure. The only unpleasant task the COIN cannot help with is doing household chores. No wonder coolfarmers are happy!

Happiness researchers are also finding that as individuals we are happier if we can help other people, or express our gratitude to other people. Interestingly, after having reached a certain level of comfort, people do not get happier if they accumulate more wealth. Your average billionaire is not happier than a moderately well-off person! Generally, people are happy if they have more than the people against whom they compare themselves. This explains why the East Germans were happier before the Berlin Wall came down, although in absolute terms they had much less in the communist days than they do today. In the old days, compared to other Eastern Europeans in Poland or Bulgaria, they were well-off. After German unification, they became the poor relatives. Although in absolute numbers East Germans had more than they had before, in comparison to their West German cousins, they now had less.

In a project at the University of Rotterdam[6] in the Netherlands, researchers found that the Danes and Swiss are the happiest people, while people in Ukraine, Zimbabwe, and Tanzania are the least happy. Out of 95 nations assessed, the United States, one of the wealthiest countries, only ranked seventeenth in happiness. Why? While per-capita income in the United States is higher than that of Denmark or Switzerland, income is far less evenly distributed and the Danes and the Swiss take much better care of their underprivileged citizens. Denmark and Switzerland even have kind of a negative income tax, where, if somebody has an income below the poverty line, not only do they not have to pay taxes, but they even obtain additional compensation payments from the state.

It therefore seems that the smaller the differences in happiness among different groups of the population, the happier the population is as a whole. What this means is that a society that takes care of everybody is much happier. If the society is very stratified, meaning that there are different levels of society with different privileges and different levels of wealth, this makes the society as a whole less happy. Taking care of the swarm is a good thing. The caretakers will be much happier people that way, too.

COOLFARMING LESSON: Every COIN member deserves fair treatment and respect.

As COINs have a meritocratic work culture, where everybody is treated fairly, they provide a highly collaborative work environment. Roles of people in COINs are based on their skills and capabilities and, thanks to the transparency of the Internet, are visible to everybody, thus leading to a happier work environment.

COOLFARMING LESSON: Make COIN members masters of their own destinies.

Another reason the Swiss are happier than most is that they feel more in control of their own destiny. Switzerland has one of the most direct democracies, where citizens vote many times a year at the national, state, and local level on a plethora of subjects. By comparison, in U.S. democracy, citizens generally only elect people as their representatives, but do not influence actions directly, *except for the occasional referendum.* Sure, U.S. citizens can write letters to their senator, but there is no guarantee that the senator will vote the way they want. In a direct democracy, citizens can take things in their own hands, vote the way they want, or even start a referendum to ask for a citizens' vote on issues they want to get changed. COINs function very much like the Swiss-style democracy, with people making their own decisions and taking their destinies into their own hands.

Conclusions for swarm businesses and collaborative innovation networks are obvious: Being happy is one of the main motivators for collaborating in a COIN. As long as COIN members are happy, they will stay with the swarm and deliver superb work. Take care of the swarm, delegate power to the swarm, let swarm members decide! When there is a happy and high-performing swarm, then you, as the instigator of the swarm, will reach your goal and be happy, too.

Coolfarmers Are Altruistic

To figure out why coolfarmers are altruistic, let's look once more at the bees. Bee researchers disagree why the individual bee puts the hive's interests and welfare before her own, in the end even sacrificing her own life for the swarm, if need be. One theory is based in evolution: The bee increases her gene pool's chances of survival through her own sacrifice. The alternative explanation simply says that an individual bee puts the interest of the hive ahead of everything because this in the end will also be good for her: A well-functioning swarm is the most supportive environment a bee can wish for. While I am no expert on bees, the second explanation makes lots of sense for human coolfarmers. They understand that the best way to reach their personal goals is to put the goals of their swarm ahead of their own interests because, in the end, it will also be most beneficial for each individual member of the swarm, too.

We adore altruistic behavior of role models. Why is it that *Harry Potter* took the world by storm and became a global phenomenon in just a few years? The reason is that Joanne Rowling did such a great job painting Harry as a perfect role model—a trendsetter—for the target group of tweens and teenagers. Harry is "one of them" and a role model the teens all strive to be. He is at the same time an underdog who has to fight to survive and the most admired boy in his wizarding community. He is human with all his defects and weaknesses, but he is also unbelievably brave and courageous, protecting the weak and trying to make the world a better place by ridding it of evil Lord Voldemort. In short, his behavior has altruistic elements. In a swarming world, Harry Potter's altruistic behavior offers a model for leadership. The interesting thing is that such behavior is not only rewarded in the fantasy world of J. K. Rowling, but has been shown to be successful in daily life, too.

In a series of mathematical modeling experiments, Harvard professor Martin Nowak[7] found that altruism indeed pays. Darwinism explains why siblings help each other, improving the chances of survival for their gene pool. But Nowak found higher success for collaborating individuals in direct reciprocity, indirect reciprocity, and network reciprocity. In a series of games, he found that if people punished each other for real or imaginary foul play, this in the end would lead to everybody being worse off. In the long term, more forgiving people also did better for themselves. Explicitly focusing on altruism, Nowak demonstrated that cooperating societies, where group members put the well-being of their entire group before their individual welfare, did significantly better than selfish communities, while at the same time also leading to higher welfare of the individual group members.

There is an impressive list of celebrities who instinctively have applied Nowak's finding to their own personal behavior. When Apple launched a new iPod model, the iPod Red, it enlisted Bono and Oprah to launch the products.[8] Both Bono and Oprah are familiar voices of the disadvantaged. U2 singer Bono is one of the most well-known pop stars who uses his fame to help the developing world. Oprah Winfrey has helped abused children, set up inner-city schools, improved learning, and gotten the American population back to reading. Apple hopes that by associating itself with these icons and their efforts to do good, the altruistic flavor rubs off on Apple products and consumers. And Apple is not alone. Motorola worked with Bono and Oprah to launch a special Red edition of its Razr mobile phone, leveraging the same association of doing good while selling a hot product.

Actors Brad Pitt and Angelina Jolie are also well known for their efforts to make our world a better place. They have not only personally adopted children from war-torn Africa, but Angelina is also a Goodwill Ambassador for the UN Refugee Agency. Roger Federer, arguably one of the best tennis players ever, is not only known for the excellence of his play, but also for his engagement to help others. He is not just a role model of fair play and good manners, but is also heavily involved in campaigns to help the disadvantaged and the poor. The engagement of these celebrities to make the world a better place also works to their personal advantage. Through their commitment to save our planet and help the disadvantaged, Bono, Oprah, Brad, Angelina, and Roger increase the value of their own brand. This means that they also improve their own bottom line, commanding a higher price for their participation in corporate marketing campaigns.

For an example of how nonaltruistic behavior is bad for everybody, let's go once more to Africa. The outcome of the 2007 Kenyan presidential elections illustrates what happens if the principle "to gain power one needs to give away power" is violated. While far from being perfect, until recently Kenya had been one of the brighter spots in the otherwise long list of corrupt black African countries. But then, incumbent Kenyan president Mwai Kibaki, through clear fraud, cheated and claimed a majority of the votes. This election fraud provoked tribal warfare when the voters, cheated out of their victory, now asked for their rights through force, leading to a bloodbath among the members of the same tribe as Kibaki. Had Kibaki given away power, and the majority of the voters been willing to give in to some sort of power-sharing arrangement, all parties in Kenya would have been much better off.

COOLFARMING LESSON: Altruistic behavior of COIN members is for their own benefit, as well as the benefit of others.

In societies with high levels of altruism, where people put the good of society before their own selfish needs, interpersonal trust is high. The good thing about high levels of trust is that it reduces transaction cost. In a society with high levels of trust there is no need for a sophisticated and costly law-enforcement system. This has been shown in a simulation experiment by academics Iris Bohnet and Bruno Frey. In a fascinating experiment,[9] they found that contracts with either very high levels of trust or very low levels of trust had a higher chance of being kept than contracts done under intermediate levels of trust. In other words, if somebody would be strongly punished, or not punished at all, the chances for a contract to be kept were the best. This finding translates directly to either (1) a situation such as in the old communist countries that meted out draconian punishment if contracts were not kept, which led to people generally keeping them, or (2) a situation like in a Finnish village where everybody knows everybody and punishment for breach of contract is replaced by shaming.

I had the chance to compare the different levels of trust in society in Switzerland and Ghana, when I was shipping used computers from Switzerland to Ghanaian schools. Shipping fifteen donated computers from Zurich to the port of Accra cost me about $800. Getting the computers out of the port of Accra cost me another $700, including hiring a handling agent, whom I needed, I was told, to manage the complexities of the port process. The rest of the money was spent for clearing fees of the shipping company, the warehouse, customs, and other various fees. The process of getting the computers released took five days of walking from one official and office to the next, accompanied by an employee of the handling agent. The process was designed to make it hard to cheat on the various fees imposed by the state. This example illustrates that transaction costs are disproportionally higher in a low-trust society such as Ghana. Increasing intersocietal trust would greatly increase the efficiency of the Ghanaian business life.

The microloans of the Grameen Bank, founded by Nobel Peace Prize winner Muhammad Yunus, are based on the principles of mutual trust. Lenders have no collateral to put down, but will be publicly shamed by losing face if they default on their loan. The more Gemeinsinn and Yhteisöllisyys a community has, the higher trust within the community will be. The more leeway members of a community have—the more trust the community gives to them—the more concerned the members of a community will be about violating this trust. But once members are let in, collaboration inside the community will be extremely efficient. Altruistic behavior is beneficial not only to societies, but also to business.

Danish heating and cooling equipment manufacturer Danfoss proves that the same altruistic principles can be highly profitable in business. Danfoss has been in this market for more than seventy years, but over the years it has taken a more and more community-oriented approach, repositioning itself as a leader of sustainable technologies, with stellar success. It is adamant about catering to the needs of all stakeholders, shareholders, employees, customers, and the rest of the world. It even offers a lush experimental science park, called the "Danfoss Universe," where everybody can learn about technical and scientific phenomena relevant to Danfoss, providing invaluable user feedback to the company. Danfoss uses this park to run innovation seminars for its own employees as well as for customers such as LEGO. In a playful environment similar to the Museum of Science in Boston, technical phenomena employed by Danfoss products are explained to children in an easy way. The same experiments are then also used to creatively inspire Danfoss engineers.

> **COOLFARMING LESSON: The higher the level of trust within a COIN, the more efficiently it operates.**

What a great way to combine altruism, in the form of sponsoring this science park for children, with an extremely creative way to develop new products for the company. This shows again that investing in altruistic actions also pays dividends to the investor.

For a negative example, look at the car industry, where GM bonds have gotten junk status while Toyota has become the most valuable car company in the world. GM placed its bets on gas-guzzling Hummers and SUVs to optimize short-term profits for itself, while driving pleasure for macho Hummer drivers. At the same time, Toyota positioned itself as a leader in green technologies and alternative energy sources. Over the last few years, GM's short-term egoistic attitude has been disastrous. On the other hand, Toyota's commitment to the environment and green technologies and sustainability has paid off very well. More recently, Toyota got some dents by investing in large trucks, particularly the Tundra model. But unlike GM, Toyota has taken swift action, diverting resources from the Tundra to producing more of its hybrid vehicles. Once more, doing good for the environment by producing environmentally sustainable products has a very positive impact on the bottom line of the investor.

> **COOLFARMING LESSON: Take care of the community.**
> As we have now seen, altruistic behavior benefits everybody in a society. Exemplary COIN members such as Linus Torvalds or Tim Berners-Lee have indeed consistently shown high levels of altruism. But altruism is beneficial for everybody in the swarm, not just the core COIN members. Low transaction costs, efficient communication, willingness to share information, and high levels of trust are cornerstones of efficient COINs.

Our villages, towns, and cities are natural human swarms. Today we have a growing tendency to congregate in huge traffic-congested cities. If one looks at development over the last fifty years, a rapidly growing fraction, already a majority by some accounts, is living in those urban centers. So we have no choice but to make those spaces more livable by recreating local neighborhoods in big cities. Supported by Internet-based tools like social networking, we can find and collaborate with "people like us" in the midst of the millions of people in Manhattan or Manila.

Swarm creativity and self-organization have an unsurpassed ability to help make the world a better place. Given the nature of the daunting challenges facing us—population growth, global hunger, religious intolerance, climate change, and political, ideological, and cultural clashes—humanity needs all the help it can get. Swarm creativity,

COINs, and coolfarming raise new opportunities for deep and far-reaching change. As an incurable optimist, I hope that if not today, then at least a few generations from now, everybody will be the master of their own destiny and happiness. As we have just seen, happiness comes from self-determination and the feeling of being in control of one's own future—and it is made even better if individuals can decide for themselves what swarm to join, and then get actively engaged in redefining and shaping the goals of their swarm.

Afterword

It's Not Chief Executives but Chief Creators We Need!

WHILE THE LEADERS of today's companies are still called chief executive officers (CEOs), leaders of COIN-based organizations should better be called *chief creative officers* (CCOs). CEOs put their emphasis on execution, not on creation. They hire management consultants to create their new strategies for them, which they then "execute." CEOs have obtained their MBAs from top-ranked business schools in the United States or Europe, where they were taught management and leadership. This means that they all lead in the same way, following the "best practices," blueprints, and rules that were hammered into their heads at business school. There, they were asked to study zillions of "case studies" of how the most successful among them did things "the right way." Not surprisingly, they were like lemmings, following management gurus and each other into the abyss of the 2008 financial crisis, teetering along and pulling each other down to the brink of bankruptcy.

I envision a totally different style of leadership. This new style of leadership is based not on "best practices," not on cookbook recipes of how to do it *one* right way, but on creativity—individual creativity and swarm creativity. The step I am proposing is a bold one: It means empowering individual people at the company, instead of amassing all the power in the hands of the chief executive who is also the chief executor. In this new type of organization there is no chief executor anymore because this role has been given away to all the stakeholders in the company. Stakeholders are the employees, the customers, the suppliers, and yes, also the management of the company. The managers are not CEOs anymore, but they are CCOs. Being highly creative themselves, they stand out by unleashing the creativity of their swarm—their employees, their lead users, their customers, and anybody they touch through their vision and products.

Let's look at the leaders who stand out today, such as Apple's Steve Jobs, Craig Newmark at Craigslist, the founders of Google, or Oprah Winfrey. All of them lead highly successful businesses that have been resilient so far in the toxic economic climate that followed the 2008 financial crisis. None of them came up the conventional management way. They were never the CEOs of their companies in the conventional sense, never the chief executors. Rather, they are the chief creators of their respective enterprises. They might have assumed the CEO title to make themselves more recognizable in their role to the rest of the world, but they did not execute somebody else's strategy.

They have created radically new products and built real, sustainable value by doing what they thought would be the right thing, listening first and foremost to themselves and to their swarm. Instead of listening to management gurus, business school professors, and strategy consultants, these leaders do not just listen, but immerse themselves in their swarm.

While conventional businesses like Motorola, GM, Ford, and Chrysler, not to mention the once mighty banks of Wall Street, are foundering, the businesses of these creators are thriving. Leaders like Oprah or Steve Jobs are not afraid to go to the front line every day. When Steve Jobs started Apple, instead of obtaining an MBA, he immersed himself in his swarm. He first listened to what others had to say, visiting world-famous Xerox PARC to learn about the computer mouse and hitching a job at an early computer company to learn even more, until he had figured it out and was ready to start building his own computers and his own company.

Chief creators also give back to their swarm. Google famously encourages its employees to be creative and come up with new products, which are then given away for free in some form until the company has figured out a way of making money from them. Google acquired photo-sharing website Picasa, set up the social networking community Orkut, and converted a start-up into Google Docs, the web-enabled office suite—all available for free to the end-user. When Steve Jobs's swarm of fanatic iPhone owners complained about a new price cut, he immediately gave back the difference in price to anybody who had bought the iPhone at the original higher price.

In short, chief creative officers, unlike CEOs, immerse themselves in their swarm; they share with their swarm and go where their swarm wants to go. Just like great farmers, their main task as coolfarmer is to provide a nurturing environment and let the swarm do the rest by and for itself.

CHAPTER 1

1. Steve Lohr, "One Day You're Indispensable, the Next Day…," *New York Times*, Jan. 18, 2009,
http://www.nytimes.com/2009/01/18/weekinreview/18lohr.html?th&emc=th.

2. IDC, "Linux Operating Systems Market Grows in 2008, Long Term Prospects Remain Good, IDC Study Finds," press release, Aug. 26, 2009, http://idc.com/getdoc.jsp?containerId=prUS21982209

CHAPTER 2

1. Eric Bonabeau, Marco Dorigo, and Guy Theraulaz, *Swarm Intelligence: From Natural to Artificial Systems: A Volume in Santa Fe Institute Studies in the Sciences of Complexity* (New York: Oxford University Press, 1999).

2. Jared Diamond, *Guns, Germs, and Steel: The Fates of Human Societies* (New York: W. W. Norton, 1999).

3. O. Raz and P. Gloor, "Size Really Matters—New Insights for Start-Up's Survival," *Management Science*, 53, no 2 (Feb. 2007), 169–177

4. Tom Allen and Ornit Raz, "The dynamics of communication patterns within a biotech cluster: A simple method for studying a complex relationship," *International Journal of Technology and Innovation Management Education*, 2 (2007), http://www.senatehall.com/technology-and-innovation-management?article=256

5. Peter Gloor and Scott Cooper, "The New Principles of a Swarm Business," *Sloan Management Review* 48, no. 3 (Spring 2007), 81–84.

6. "Craig (of the List) Looks Beyond the Web," *New York Times*, May 12, 2008, http://www.nytimes.com/2008/05/12/technology/12craig.html? pagewanted=2&th&adxnnl=1&emc=th&adxnnlx=1210599228 QH4YFXik6rWCCP/yIeRzmA.

7. "Turbo-Bienen Lenken den Schwarm" (Turbo Bees Guide the Swarm) *Spiegel*, Oct. 4, 2008, http://www.spiegel.de/wissenschaft/natur/0,1518,582107,00.html.

8. Map of World Happiness—A Global Projection of Subjective Well-Being, http://www.technovelgy.com/ct/Science-Fiction-News.asp?NewsNum=893.

CHAPTER 3

1. "Linus Torvalds: A Very Brief and Completely Unauthorized Biography," www.linfo.org/linus.html (accessed Nov. 15, 2008).

2. Gary Rivlin, "Leader of the Free World: How Linus Torvalds became benevolent dictator of Planet Linux, the biggest collaborative project in history," *Wired*, http://www.wired.com/wired/archive/11.11/linus_pr.html.

3. Rivlin, "Leader of the Free World."

4. "Linus Torvalds' Benevolent Dictatorship," *BusinessWeek*, Aug. 18, 2004, http://www.businessweek.com/technology/content/aug2004/tc20040818_1593 _PG2.htm.

5. Nelson D. Schwartz, "C.E.O. Evolution Phase 3," *New York Times*, Nov. 10, 2007, http://www.nytimes.com/2007/11/10/business/10leaders.html?_r=1 &em&ex=1194843600&en=5991d1898d96b957&ei=5087%0A&oref=slogin.

6. "Linus Torvalds," Knoppix Documentation Wiki, http://www.knoppix.net/wiki/Linus_Torvalds (accessed Aug. 20, 2008).

7. Stephen Shankland, "Torvalds: A Solaris skeptic," Cnet news, Dec. 21, 2004, http://news.cnet.com/Torvalds-a-Solaris-skeptic/2008-1082_3- 5498799.html.

8. Thomas A. Bass, "Being Nicholas: The Wired Interview," http://archives.obs-us.com/obs/english/books/nn/bd1101bn.htm.

9. Bass, "Being Nicholas."

10. "Person of the Week: Nicholas Negroponte," ABC News, Nov. 18, 2005, http://abcnews.go.com/WNT/PersonOfWeek/story?id=1327028.

11. "Person of the Week: Nicholas Negroponte," ABC News.

12. Daniel Hernandez, "To See and Be Scene," *Los Angeles Times*, Oct. 25, 2005, http://articles.latimes.com/2005/oct/25/local/me-cobrasnake25.

13. Hernandez, "To See and Be Scene," *Los Angeles Times*.

14. Shawn Hubler, "The Secret Life of Cory Kennedy," *Los Angeles Times*, Feb. 25, 2007, http://articles.latimes.com/2007/feb/25/magazine/tm- corykennedy08.

15. Linus Torvalds' Benevolent Dictatorship, *BusinessWeek.*

CHAPTER 4

1. Kenneth Rexroth, "The Cubist Poetry of Pierre Reverdy," http://www.bopsecrets.org/rexroth/essays/reverdy.htm.essay (accessed Nov. 6, 2009); originally published as the Introduction to Rexroth's translation of *Pierre Reverdy's Selected Poems* (New York: New Directions, 1969).

2. Jason P. Davis and Kathleen M. Eisenhardt, "Rotating Leadership and Symbiotic Organization: Relationships Processes in the Context of Collaborative Innovation," Working paper, MIT Sloan School of Management.

3. Davis and Eisenhardt, "Rotating Leadership."

4. Ibid.

5. Emanuel Lazega, et al., "Catching up with big fish in the big pond? Multi-level network analysis through linked design," *Social Networks* 30 no. 2 (2008), 159–176.

CHAPTER 5

1. Masamichi Takahashi, et al., "The Shift from Centralized to Peer-to-Peer Communication in an Online Community: Participants as a Useful Aspect of Genre Analysis" (MIT Center for Collective Intelligence [CCI] working paper 2008-001, MIT Sloan School of Management working paper 4677-08).

2. "The Online Fan World of the Twilight Vampire Books," *BusinessWeek*, July 31, 2008, http://www.businessweek.com/magazine/content/08_32/b4095044373786.htm?chan=search.

3. "Online Fan World of the Twilight Vampire Books," *BusinessWeek.*

CHAPTER 6

1. Brendan I. Koerner, "Geeks in Toyland," *Wired* 14.02 (Feb. 2006), http://www.wired.com/wired/archive/14.02/lego.html?pg=1&topic=lego&topic_set=.

2. Presentation by Lewis Pinault, LEGO, at Rezonance conference, Geneva, June 18, 2008

3. P. Gloor, *Swarm Creativity: Competitive Advantage Through Collaborative Innovation Networks* (New York: Oxford University Press, 2006).

CHAPTER 7

1. M. DiMaggio, P. Gloor, and G. Passiante, "Collaborative Innovation Networks, Virtual Communities, and Geographical Clustering," in "Intelligent Clusters, Communities and Cities: Enhancing innovation with virtual environments and embedded systems," special issue, *International*

Journal of Innovation and Regional Development, 1 no. 4 (2009), 387–404; O. Raz and P. Gloor, "Size Really Matters—New Insights for Start-Up's Survival," *Management Science*, 53 no. 2 (Feb. 2007), 169–177; and P. Gloor, et al., "Finding Collaborative Innovation Networks Through Correlating Performance with Social Network Structure," *Journal of Production Research*, 46 no. 5 (Apr. 2007), 1357–1371.

2. Peter Gloor, et al., "Web Science 2.0: Identifying Trends Through Semantic Social Network Analysis," Proceedings IEEE Conference on Social Computing (SocialCom-09), Aug 29–31, 2009, Vancouver.

3. Condor was originally developed at MIT and Dartmouth College and is still free for academic use (www.ickn.org). It is marketed commercially by software start-up galaxyadvisors (www.galaxyadvisors.com).

4. J. Krauss, et al., "Predicting Movie Success and Academy Awards Through Sentiment and Social Network Analysis," in Proceedings of the 16th European Conference on Information Systems, June 9–11, 2008, Galway, Ireland.

5. "Top 100 Public Intellectuals," *Foreign Policy*, May 2008, http://www.foreignpolicy.com/story/cms.php?story_id=4314.

6. P. Gloor, et al., "Studying Microscopic Peer-to-Peer Communication Patterns," in Proceedings of the AMCIS (Americas Conference on Information Systems), Aug. 9–12, 2007, Keystone, CO.

7. Alex (Sandy) Pentland, *Honest Signals: How They Shape Our World* (Cambridge, MA: MIT Press, 2008).

CHAPTER 8

1. "FM Interview with Linus Torvalds: What motivates free software developers," *First Monday*, 3 no. 3 (March 2, 1998), http://firstmonday.org/htbin/cgiwrap/bin/ojs/index.php/fm/article/view/583/504.

2. Francis Fukuyama, *Trust: The Social Virtues and the Creation of Prosperity* (New York: Free Press Simon & Schuster, 1995).

3. The Ken Lay e-mails are analyzed in-depth in the author's previous book, Peter Gloor and Scott Cooper, *Coolhunting: Chasing Down the Next Big Thing* (New York: AMACOM, 2007).

4. Remi Trudel and June Cotte, "Does Being Ethical Pay?" *Sloan Management Review*, May 2008, http://sloanreview.mit.edu//wsj/insight/brand/2008/05/12/.

5. Bruno S. Frey and Simon Luechinger, "Concepts of Happiness and Their Measurement," Metropolis-Verlag, Marburg, July 2007.

6. World Database of Happiness, http://www1.eur.nl/fsw/happiness/index.html.

7. Martin Nowak, "Five Rules for the Evolution of Cooperation," *Science*, 314 no. 5805 (December 8, 2006).

8. Tom Krazit, "Bono, Oprah, and a Red iPod?" Cnet news, Oct. 12, 2006, http://news.cnet.com/8301-10784_3-6125446-7.html.

9. Iris Bohnet, Bruno Frey, and Steffen Huck. "More order with less law: On contract enforcement, trust, and crowding," *American Political Science Review*, 95 no. 1 (March 2001), 131–44.

Silk Road, 33
Slackware, 26
Slashdot, 26, 54
social badges, 181–184
social networks
  actions of people using social
    badges, 181–184
  blogs, 163, 167, 168–174, 187
  collaboration through, 202
  collaborative innovation through,
    150–155
  coolfarming and, 186–190
  Internet Movie Database (IMDB),
    167, 178–179
Solaris, 78–79
Soroush, Abdolkarim, 176
Stallman, Richard, 23, 24
Starbucks, 3
Stein, Gertrude, 104
stock trends, 180
subprime mortgage crisis, 37–38,
  206
success, advertising, 128–129, 132
Sugar operating system, 83
Sun Microsystems, 20, 22, 78–79
SUSE, 26
swarm businesses, 70–71
swarm creativity, 3
  in bee swarming, 10–11, 30, 32–33,
    40–55
  benefits of, 39–40
  "black swans" versus, 37–40
  communication in, 34–37, 65,
    101–102
  consequences, 31–32
  effectiveness of, 66–67
  in Ghana, 55–66, 88–98
  growth of, 20
  individual creativity versus, 206
  LEGO Mindstorms, 29–30, 43
  Linux, 29–30, 49, 81–82
  member characteristics, 30
  nature of, 30
  public transportation by, 58–59,
    61–64
  self-organization and, 202–203
  sharing with swarm and, 67–68,
    95–98, 99

swarm business, defined, 38–39
  World Wide Web and, 29–30, 45
swarm intelligence, 32
Swiffer Duster, 127
Swiss Deloitte, 152–153
Switzerland, 189, 195–196

Taleb, Nassim Nicholas, 37–38, 163
Tanenbaum, Andrew, 22–24
Target, 147
Technology Entrepreneurs (Procter &
  Gamble), 124–129, 133
  embedding in business units, 126
  internally developed ideas, 126
telecommunications, 6, 36
telegraph, 6
Tesla, Nikola, 5–6
Thompson, Ken, 21
3M, 125
Tolstoy, Leo, 136
Torvalds, Linus, 23–28, 44, 45, 49,
  73–75, 78, 80–81, 86–87,
  185–186, 202
Toulouse-Lautrec, Henri de, 103
tourism, coolfarming in Ghana, 88–93,
  98–99
Toyota, 201–202
transparency, 191, 193
trendsetters, 7–9, 53–54
Trudel, Remi, 191–192
trust
  balloon pilots and, 75–77
  power over people and, 75,
    199–200
Ts'o, Ted, 25, 49
Tucker, Adam, 144
Twilight book series, 129–132
Twilight Lexicon, 131–132
Twilight MOMS, 131–132

UBS, 20–21, 38
Ubuntu, 26
Unicharm, 127
University of California, Berkeley,
  21–22
University of Rotterdam, 195
University of Zurich, 22
Unix, 21, 22–23, 78–79

ABOUT THE AUTHOR

Peter A. Gloor is a Research Scientist at the Center for Collective Intelligence at MIT's Sloan School of Management where he leads a project exploring Collaborative Innovation Networks. He is also Founder and Chief Creative Officer of software startup galaxyadvisors, where he puts his academic insights to practical use helping clients to coolhunt by analyzing social networking patterns on the Internet—and spot the next big thing by finding the trendsetters, and to coolfarm—making the cool trends succeed on online social networking sites.

He is also Mercator Visiting Professor at the University of Cologne, and a lecturer at Aalto University in Helsinki. Previously, Peter was a Partner with Deloitte Consulting, leading its e-Business practice for Europe, a Partner with PricewaterhouseCoopers, and the section leader for software engineering at UBS. He was a postdoctoral fellow at the MIT Lab for Computer Science in the Advanced Networking Architecture group, working on hypertext well before the Web emerged. He obtained a Ph.D in computer science from the University of Zurich in 1989 and a Master's degree in mathematics in 1986, also from the University of Zurich.

In his spare time he likes to work on bridging the digital divide by bringing computers to Africa, hiking and skiing in the mountains, and playing the piano.